Waking Up Together *is an insp[...]* *spirituality and relationships. L[...]* *that can help couples navigate [...]* *dynamics of relationships. By asking the central questions—What are we waking up from? and, What are we waking into?—Baggett has named a central issue for couples who want to deepen their own spiritual work in the context of committed relationships. Recognizing, defining, and naming the importance of unconscious and conscious trances and their role in relationships is one of the central ideas in the book that can inspire couples into a practice that will allow an ever deepening commitment to the awakening joy and beauty inherent in all conscious relationships. I highly recommend this book and will use in my classes at Holistic Studies.*

—Ray Greenleaf, Chair, Counseling Psychology, School of Holistic Studies, John F. Kennedy University

I sure could have used Chip Baggett's book in my journey, half asleep, through the marriage swamps and jungles. Waking up is hard enough for one person. Baggett wisely and enticingly offers ways for couples to wake up from trances and connect as real, conscious people. Sleep-walkers don't know they are sleep-walking. Do you? Let Baggett confront and guide you into consciousness as an individual and a partner. This is a welcome wake-up nudge.

—Tom Greening Ph.D., Professor of Psychology, Saybrook Graduate School; Clinical Professor, UCLA

Perhaps the reason the divorce rate is so high is because too many people are "asleep" in their relationships, reliving dysfunctional patterns from the past without being conscious of it. Chip Baggett invites us to awaken from the trances of our lives to create relationship as conscious, living process. By becoming emotionally and spiritually present in our relationships, we can consciously grow the soul connection we desire in our heart of hearts. Chip Baggett gives us the roadmap and the steps along the way."

—Linda Marks, author of *Healing the War Between the Genders: The Power of the Soul-Centered Relationship* and *Living With Vision: Reclaiming the Power of the Heart*

Powerfully written, Waking Up Together *is an important contribution for clinicians and couples involved in illumination and true change at the deepest level. Baggett provides an elegant approach to couples therapy, both timely and timeless.*

—Dr. David Quillian, Atlanta Center for Cognitive Therapy

Waking Up Together *offers couples a deeply compassionate, psychologically astute, and spiritually informed path. Having been exposed to a variety of approaches in our careers as psychotherapists, this is the one we use in our own relationship. Elegant in its simplicity, easy to understand, and it works!*
—Lisa Gould, MSW and David Gould, MSW

Waking Up Together *is a must-have book for couples who want to take their relationship to a new and exciting level. Baggett lays out, in clear and concise terms, what causes relationships to fail while outlining the tools needed to jettison the old habits (trances) responsible for potential failures. He shines new light on relationship dynamics that make perfect sense once recognized. There are so many aha's in this little book you will wish you had found it years ago.* —Lynn Wortman, RN and J. J. Wortman, Ph.D.

While I have long thought of myself as a spiritual seeker, the relationship with my wife is turning out to provide the most significant waking up power yet, and it has been right under my nose all along. —R.T.

Chip's work has finally given me, at the age of 63, the concrete tools to heal myself and to heal my relationship. As I work this process, I feel free of old patterns and connected to myself, my partner, my community, and my world. —E.E.

When I was introduced to Chip's work and the principles in his book, I felt HOPE for myself and my relationship. In my 62 years of living and doing therapy, I have never been shown the key that has now unlocked and freed me from myself—my egoic trances. Deep gratitude to Chip and his insights.
—K.C.

Being able to recognize when either my wife or I go into a trance has been instrumental in freeing our relationship of reaction, hurt, and blame. We were heading towards ending our 20-year marriage. Now, having gained the awareness of how trances influence our daily lives, we have broken through our old behavior patterns and our relationship is flourishing in new and unexpected ways."
—R.T.

VOLUME ONE

Waking Up *Together*

AN INTERACTIVE PRACTICE FOR COUPLES

Leland Baggett

Foreword by David N. Elkins, Ph.D.

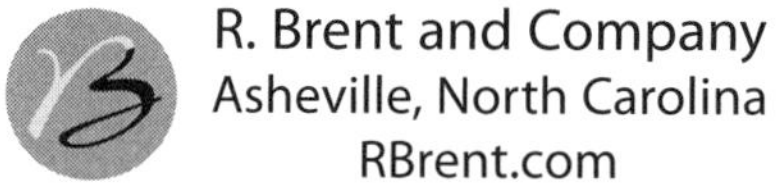
R. Brent and Company
Asheville, North Carolina
RBrent.com

WAKING UP TOGETHER: AN INTERACTIVE PRACTICE FOR COUPLES.
Copyright © 2009 by Leland G. Baggett, III. All rights reserved.
Reproduction and translation of any part of this work beyond that permitted by Sections 107 and 108 of the United States Copyright Act without the permission of the copyright owners is unlawful.

Published in Asheville, North Carolina
by R. Brent and Company
50 Deerwood Drive
Asheville NC 28805
828–299–0977
RBrent.com

Editor and publisher: *Robbin Brent Whittington*
Cover design: *jb graphics, Asheville NC*
Interior design and Composition: *Rick Soldin, Jonesborough TN*
Author photograph: © *2009 by R.L. Geyer*

Library of Congress Cataloging-in-Publication Data

Baggett III, Leland G.
Waking up together: an interactive practice for couples—1st ed.
p. cm.
ISBN-13: 978-0-9788160-5-6
1. Relationships—Psychology. 2. Relationships—Spiritual life.
3. Conscious Living. 4. Self-help.
1. Title
2009932046

First Edition

14 13 12 11 10 09 1 2 3 4 5

Printed in the United States of America

In loving memory of Bob Avinash Markman

Teacher, healer, and friend who touched so many lives with his humble, loving, passionate presence. He was a man who found the sweet nectar of being awake irresistible.
And he loved to write Haiku.

The truth of it all
I'm making up as I go
How do you do it?

—Avinash

Contents

Acknowledgements ix
Note from the Author xiii
Foreword xv
Introduction xvii

chapter one: Cohesive Elements of a Relationship 1
A Shared (or Compatible) Vision 2
Jessie and Patrick 3
Intrinsically Rewarding Moments 5
Complementary Dysfunctional Patterns 7

chapter two: Trance Consciousness 11
Six Characteristics of Trance States 16
Six Contexts of Trances 24

chapter three: The Entranced Relationship 29
Janet and William 30
Linda and Connie 35
Jessie and Patrick 38

chapter four: An Individual Practice of Awakening 45
Three Skills Needed for Awakening 46
Stalking Our Trances 54
Lucid Dreaming 57
Key Points of an Individual Practice 63

chapter five: A Shared Practice of Awakening 65

Level One: A Parallel Practice 66

Ellen and David 69

A Parallel Practice: Points to Remember 74

Level Two: The Interactive Practice, An Introduction 75

chapter six: An Interactive Practice, Stage One: Preparation 79

Step One: Establish Partnership of Mutual Intent 80

Step Two: Identify Parameters of Shared Trances 82

Jessie and Patrick 84

Step Three: Establish Personalized "Wake Up" Cues 87

chapter seven: An Interactive Practice, Stage Two: Application 91

Waking Up Inside the Dream 91

Lucy and Greg 94

Jessie and Patrick 98

An Interactive Practice in Perspective 105

Conclusion 107

Bibliography 109

Suggested Reading List 111

Glossary of Terms 113

Waking Up Tools at a Glance 119

Six Characteristics of Trance States 120

Key Points of an Individual Practice 122

Key Points of a Parallel Practice 123

Three Steps of an Interactive Practice of Awakening
Stage One: Preparation 124

An Interactive Practice, Stage Two: Application 126

About the Author 127

Quick Reference Guides 129

Acknowledgements

I am truly humbled when I consider who I want to acknowledge for contributing to this work. Although I began formally writing this book about four years ago, my approach to couple's therapy had been evolving for several years prior to that. The many people and ideas that have influenced my understanding about life and love and relationship—not to mention therapy with couples—could be its own book. That said, I will limit my comments to those who have had a direct or pivotal influence on this work in particular.

I must first thank my parents for the unending love that surrounded me, and for the specific gifts and qualities each emphasized and cultivated in me. My mother nurtured in me an artistic sensibility and a deep appreciation for aesthetic balance and order. She also instilled the value of fairness, both in play and in relationships. She taught me the importance of self-discipline, commitment, and responsibility. My father evoked a kind of earthy physicality and an intimate loving connection to nature and animals. He also stimulated in me a passion for philosophical inquiry and the cultivation of the intellectual skills needed to support that passion. He believed in me and challenged me until it became my own conviction that it was not just my right, but my responsibility to be true to myself and to live a life that reflected that integrity.

Ironically, my parents gave me another gift that I'm sure neither intended. When I was in the sixth grade, they went through an emotionally volatile divorce. In the intensity of their anguish, they each maintained their own version of the problems and circumstances that led to the end of their marriage. Their versions were in stark contradiction to each other, and were not at all consistent with my experience of either of them. Looking back, I believe it was the depth of my love for my parents in the midst of such painfully irresolvable stories that pushed me to acknowledge that my love and appreciation for who each of them truly was, was deeper and unrelated to the painful drama they both seemed to identify with at the time. This well may be the original seed of my approach to couples' therapy.

I am also exceedingly grateful for the humanistic psychology department at the University of West Georgia, created and nurtured by the late Mike Arons, Ph.D., an extraordinary visionary, educator, and human being. The program, still early in its development when I was a graduate student, was not just another psychology department but was an experiential learning community that offered a rare opportunity to combine personal growth and exploration of consciousness with the intellectual rigor of humanistic, existential, phenomenological, and transpersonal theory. The unique environment those professors and fellow students nurtured as mentors and friends thirty years ago continues to inspire my work to this day.

I would like to acknowledge one student I met in that department, Dave Quillian, a kindred soul who became a housemate, fellow band member, true friend, and colleague. Through the years, he has supported and encouraged me to write down my ideas and put them out into the world. This particular book was an outgrowth of a broader collaborative writing project that Dave and I were considering at one time.

I am also grateful for my editor/publisher, Robbin Brent Whittington of R. Brent and Company, for her belief in this work and her commitment to help me make these ideas more accessible. Her respect for my voice as a writer, her keen eye for both the detail and the whole picture, and her constant challenge that I stretch, clarify, and connect these ideas more fluidly has benefited me greatly as a writer and, I trust, will make your experience as a reader more rewarding.

My work has continued to grow, mature, and deepen in the course of my therapy practice with both individuals and couples. I am honored to have worked with such courageous and often brilliant clients, willing to go further and dig deeper to face their hurts and fears and confusions. It is their need, their willingness, and their readiness to wake up from their own suffering that compels and challenges me to show up in new ways and to keep growing professionally. The challenge and the gift of working with such individuals and couples is that it requires that I continue my own psychological and spiritual growth. Though our roles may be different, our journey into a fuller, deeper, and more awake humanness is the same.

I am blessed with a community of loving friends who are, in their own ways, committed to living awake and interpersonally authentic lives and with whom I continue to learn what it means to be in sacred community. I am also deeply grateful for my family: wild and wooly, loving and brilliant, passionate and stubborn, funny and crazy and ordinary as we are; what an amazing vessel of healing I was born into! And I must make special mention of my daughter, Carly, who has given me a gift so precious it is difficult to put into words. At the moment of her birth, when she landed in my arms and looked directly into my eyes, I discovered in the core of my heart the true experience of joyous, unconditional love. In some new and unexpected way, I discovered a whole new depth to who I was.

Last, I want to express my deep love and gratefulness to Natalie, my partner in life, love, and play in this sacred adventure together. So much of my professional work is informed by our relationship with all its ups and downs, challenges and discoveries, pain and humor, blind spots and revelations. She has tirelessly read or listened to passages in this book and has offered many helpful insights and suggestions that have made it more readable. She is fond of telling our friends that whenever she misbehaves, I get a glazed look in my eyes and then run to the computer to write another page! She threatens to write a rebuttal chapter. Maybe next time.

Note from the Author

Because this work presents what will be, for many, a radically different approach to understanding and being in a couple relationship, the initial emphasis will be on laying out a conceptual framework for how and why it works. I have included examples of individuals and couples in specific situations who represent different levels of emotional maturity and personal awareness.

In addition, since most of us experience our own relationship in the ongoing story of our lives, I have included a more elaborate and textured example of one fictional couple, Jessie and Patrick. They are a composite of very real aspects of a variety of individuals and couples I have known, either in my private life, or in my work as a psychotherapist. Their story will gradually unfold and be interwoven into the conceptual ideas as they are developed throughout the book.

It is my hope that you, the reader, will grow more comfortable and able to move easily from the conceptual to the imaginal and back again as you progress through these pages. Getting the "look and feel" of how a couple might work with these ideas should make it easier to translate into your own personal life and relationship journey.

—Leland "Chip" Baggett
Summer 2009
Asheville, North Carolina

Foreword

I first met Leland "Chip" Baggett more than 15 years ago at a meeting of the Association for Humanistic Psychology. I was immediately impressed by his quick mind, thoughtful approach to life, and his wonderful sense of humor. I am deeply honored that he invited me to write the foreword for his book.

Waking Up Together: An Interactive Practice for Couples is a unique book that draws on humanistic, existential, and transpersonal psychology, and incorporates Eastern ideas such as meditation and waking up. The author seamlessly joins these disciplines into an integrated approach to working with couples that is both practical and profound.

Far too many approaches to couples therapy are based on either a mechanical or medical model of human relationships. In the mechanical model the therapist, like an automobile mechanic, identifies the problems and tries to fix them so the relationship will run more smoothly. In the medical model the therapist, like a family physician, attempts to diagnose the "pathology" that lies at the core of the relational difficulties and then "administers techniques" to "cure" the pathology.

Thankfully, *Waking Up Together* is not based on either of these models. I say "thankfully" because it is my strong opinion that the last thing we need is yet another book on how to "fix" our relationships or "cure" our relational pathologies. What we do need—and what Chip Baggett delivers—is a book that tells us how to transform our relationships so that they become spiritual incubators for the growth and development of each partner. So if you are looking for a "fix" or a "cure," you should lay this book aside because here you will find neither. But if you would like to transform your relationship and make it truly extraordinary, that possibility awaits you in the following pages. In contrast to fixes and cures, this book offers a "growth and transformation" model of human relationships. Its author challenges us to "wake up" from our old, stifling patterns and to move toward a deeper, more fulfilling way of being together.

Finally, I am pleased that Chip had the courage to place spirituality at the center of his approach. Carl Jung once said that he could help only those midlife patients who had recovered a spiritual orientation to life. In a similar vein, Martin Buber said while techniques may be of some value, we can only heal the core of the person through relationship. In *Waking Up Together*, Chip Baggett reminds us that authentic, transformative relationships are spiritual in nature. In order to touch and support our partner, and truly heal our relationship, we must be in soul-to-soul contact. And to be in soul-to-soul contact means that we must also be in contact with our own soul. We can reach into the soul of the other only as deeply as the place from which we come within ourselves. As the existential theologian Paul Tillich said, "Depth speaks to depth."

Chip Baggett has worked with couples for many years. He has also worked with himself and his own relationships. This book is testament to his professional and personal journey. It shows that he has become a wise man with something very special to offer those who hunger for a relationship that is deep and real. If you are in that group of seekers, I suggest that you turn the page and begin reading.

David N. Elkins, Ph.D.
Professor Emeritus of Psychology
Graduate School of Education and Psychology
Pepperdine University
Core Faculty, Colorado School of Professional Psychology
University of the Rockies

Introduction

To fully grasp what it means to wake up together, we must address two integrally related questions: what are we waking up *from*? and, what we are waking up *into*? The first question is essentially a psychological one; the second is a spiritual one. Broadly speaking, what we are waking up from is the automatic, self-perpetuating, rigid patterns and diminished awareness of a conditioned mind upon which our ego identity is based. What we are waking up into is a direct and ever-growing awareness of our true Self, our spiritual essence or soul.

Just as with any life endeavor, we can engage in our personal relationships either in relatively unconscious and automatic ways, or with a clear intent to be mentally and emotionally present and spiritually awake. Most of us seem to fall somewhere in-between, with moments of heightened clarity at certain crucial times in our lives, such as during a momentous event, life passage, or a deep personal crisis. The more automatic, reactive, and unreflective we live and relate to one another, the narrower our perceptions are, and the fewer real choices we are free to make, and the more the quality of our life experience is diminished. On the other hand, the more present and aware we are, the more spontaneous, original, and creative we can be about how we live our lives. The more spiritually awake we are, the deeper and more meaningful our lives and relationships can be. The best way I know to describe and contrast these different ways of being is to share my own story of a moment of awakening.

My first clearly recognizable experience of this occurred nearly thirty years ago. That experience planted a seed of understanding that has evolved and matured over the years, and continues to inform my work to this day. At the time, I had had no prior experience of such a profound shift in consciousness. So I was taken completely by surprise when it happened spontaneously in the heat of a frustrating and painful argument between my beloved girlfriend and myself. Following is my memory of this moment.

My girlfriend (I will call her Leslie) and I had become loud and angry, stomping from room to room, challenging each other, and defending ourselves. At some point in the argument, we stopped and sat down in chairs facing each other, gearing up for yet another round. The hurt and defensiveness continued to escalate and there seemed to be no turning back. I was reacting to her anger, her accusations, and her implicit demand that I change; a demand I could feel in the way she held her body and could see in her face. I felt resentful and indignant and, with each moment, I was becoming harder and colder and more guarded.

Then, something inside me unexpectedly shifted. For some inexplicable reason, my whole defensive posture seemed in an instant to completely evaporate. It was if someone had flipped the "off" switch to the energy that had been sustaining all of my resistance. My emotional constriction and the related physical tension held in my body immediately relaxed. As this occurred, it felt completely unnecessary to continue shielding myself from the fierceness of Leslie's verbal assault. Instead, it became effortless, easy, and natural to open up inside and let her anger pass through me like wind through a screen door. I was struck with how this relieved me of any need to struggle, and how it allowed me to see us both with an uncharacteristic clarity.

> Because my shift from intense resistance to loving acceptance was so complete and so obviously real, and because I was able to be fully present to us both as the change occurred, there was nothing left between Leslie and me to feed the fight.

At once, the fortress of her anger became transparent. Behind the anger, I saw a frightened, hurt child struggling not to lose love. I felt the anguish of her desperation as she kept trying to find footing on ground that felt like quicksand. I was deeply moved by the sight of her so exposed and vulnerable. And I realized how I had been competing for that same love. I could see the intensity of my emotional demand that she acknowledge my worthiness of love, and how hurt and lost I felt when she did not.

This awareness emerged all at once, as though I had just awakened out of a torturous dream in which we had both been trapped. Freed from the dream, I found myself in an exquisitely peaceful state, filled with love for Leslie and for myself and for the whole of life. Even this seemed to deepen and expand until I felt intensely and intimately connected, not only to her, but also to a larger context of existence that was undeniably sacred and purposeful beyond anything I had ever known.

At that point, the subject of the argument, my position, even my need to be understood, all faded in importance. It was just not possible to take our melodrama seriously. I realized that Leslie and I had been stuck once again in our own self-centered demands and, more than likely, would get stuck again. Yet, I could now see that the dynamic between us was simply one of an infinite variety of expressions of spirit. The fact that we had chosen to create a particularly constricted one wasn't of great concern, once I realized it had no substantial reality beyond the moments we were entrenched in it. In that realization, I experienced no conflict, no need to react. I simply felt deep compassion for us both.

Because my shift from intense resistance to loving acceptance was so complete and so obviously real, and because I was able to be fully present to us both as the change occurred, there was nothing left between Leslie and me to feed the fight. A new possibility of trust emerged, and within moments, Leslie came to a still, calm, peaceful place.

For days afterward, I walked around almost dazed. The difference in the quality of my experience was palpable and profound. And yet, the shift was instantaneous and effortless.

Only later did I come to the realization that the gift and the grace of such an experience is intrinsic to who we all truly are, and that the principles and practices of being psychologically present and spiritually awake are universal and the benefits are profound for anyone who chooses to live with such intent. When this same intent is *central* to our primary partnered relationship, a whole new realm of opportunities will present themselves. Yet, most relationship books and workshops are not primarily focused on deep psychological presence or spiritual awakening. Rather, they usually address styles of communication, behavior change, and emotional healing (as do most therapies for relationships). Traditionally, the broad professional field of *mental health* has shied away from issues of spirituality, generally regarding such matters as beyond its scope. The spiritual aspect of a relationship may be acknowledged in general or vague terms, such as *enrichment* or *aspiration*. But even then, a kind of polarity is often implied that sets apart the spiritual dimension as secondary or peripheral to the more immediate psychological and interpersonal issues the couple is facing.

If we approach this from the other end of the polarity, we find that different spiritual and religious traditions do, in fact, support the idea of committed relationships as essentially spiritual, with marriage in particular being considered a holy union. But quite often, the emphasis is placed on the roles, behaviors, and attitudes considered appropriate to the particular religious orientation without paying sufficient attention to the complex psychological issues involved. Further, not all religious orientations embrace—or even define—the couple relationship as a dynamic path of spiritual awakening. In some cases, especially when fear and guilt play a central role in influencing behavior, we can get trapped or sidetracked by too narrow and dogmatic an interpretation of the roles and rules within a given tradition. This can actually be a hindrance to awakening. Simply believing in a religious doctrine or obeying a set of rules does not in and of itself make us, or our relationship, spiritually awake.

There seems to be a gap, or a noticeable absence—with relatively few exceptions*—of approaches to relationships that consider the souls' *journey of awakening* to be the central concern, with the dynamics of

---

*Two important exceptions are: John Welwood, who wrote *Journey of the Heart: The Path of Conscious Love* (1990), and *Love and Awakening: Discovering the Sacred Path of Intimate Relationship;* and Stephen and Ondrea Levine, who wrote *Embracing the Beloved: Relationship as a Path of Awakening* (1995).

personality and ego being addressed within that deeper, more explicitly spiritual context. This book is a response to that absence. It focuses on the couple relationship in particular as a unique and powerful vessel for profound psychological growth in the context of spiritual awakening. It shows how the couple relationship can, itself, be a spiritual path.

By "couple" I mean any partnered love relationship between two mutually committed individuals. This certainly includes, but is not limited to, conventional marriage. The traditional definitions and categories of relationship and lifestyles within any culture can hold great meaning for many but may not be the truest expressions for everyone. There are growing numbers who are experimenting with their lives, seeking to create new and alternative ways of expressing love and commitment that feel more authentic, more vital, more deeply and immediately true to their soul than they have found within the limited choices prescribed or legitimized by tradition or current convention.* While the dominant social conventions of any culture will invariably exert pressure to conform, one of the challenges of a path of spiritual awakening is to make choices from our deepest integrity rather than from social pressure, and to walk the life path truest to our soul.

One of the challenges of a path of spiritual awakening is to make choices from our deepest integrity rather than from social pressure, and to walk the life path truest to our soul.

Any couple relationship, no matter what social or legal form it takes, can be entered into as, or transformed into, a viable and potent path of spiritual awakening, if there is an honest and mutual intent to do so. Should two individuals acknowledge their relationship as essentially spiritual, they open themselves and their relationship to an infinitely larger context of being and awareness than the strictly psychosocial context in which our western culture ordinarily places us.

This larger context is both spiritual and transpersonal. It is spiritual in that it seeks to know and to embrace the sacred and the holy. It is transpersonal in that it represents an essential aspect or dimension of being that is larger, deeper and, in some sense, beyond a strictly personal,

---

*Daphne Rose Kingma examines a wide range of expressions of love in our changing culture in her book *The Future of Love: The Power of the Soul in Intimate Relationships* (1998).

local, cultural, or biological identity. Ordinary language can only approximate the nature and quality of such an aspect or dimension, and different traditions attempt to get at its essence by using words like transcendent, mystical, eternal, mythic, karmic, or even cosmic. In this context, the soul can be seen as an individualized yet inseparable expression of a larger reality, much like a wave in the ocean.

Awakening to this aspect of being should not be confused with avoiding, denying, or abdicating the nitty-gritty emotional and interpersonal challenges of our ordinary lives in favor of some ungrounded ethereal fantasy or disconnected state of consciousness. Such *spiritual bypass* is usually indicative of unresolved or un-owned psychological issues that need to be honestly faced. Avoidance of these issues is not an indication of authentic spiritual awareness. If the true nature of being human includes both psychological and spiritual aspects—a central premise of this work—then waking up as a *whole* person must necessarily embrace and include the full spectrum of both aspects.

To say that what we are waking up *from* is essentially a psychological matter is not to suggest that waking up means becoming less psychological. Rather, it means becoming directly and fluidly conscious of the psychological realm of our experience, where we tend to be dominated by the function—and limitations—of the ego. "The ego," in this sense, is essentially a sorting and selecting mechanism of consciousness, conditioned by a number of elements, such as the narrative of our life events, our family of origin, and the collective assumptions of the society in which we live. Since the ego is only a mechanism, it has no independent intelligence; it cannot love. Yet, because it functions so pervasively and constantly in the management of the endless details of our ordinary daily life, it gets most of our attention. We then tend to become ensnared and entranced in a very diminished awareness and expression of our true Self. This creates a kind of "veil of consciousness" that makes it more difficult to access a direct experience of the depth and joy, the magnificence, and the true beauty of who we are spiritually.

Truly opening in order to embrace the spiritual dimension of one's being is a deeply challenging process and is anything but an escape. As we allow ourselves to be informed by this more expansive perspective, we become far more able to honestly face the hard stuff of relationship: the hurts, the fears, the frustrations, the confusions, and the misunderstandings. We are also more able to change, heal, or truly let go of these more contracted and limiting patterns that so often seem to define and control us. Doing this in partnership with another becomes a kind of a shared mindfulness practice. It not only deepens and accelerates psychological growth individually, it creates an opportunity to wake up together spiritually, as well.

When a couple chooses to center and ground their relationship in the conscious intent to wake up, they are choosing a path that is extraordinarily rich, alive, and original; a path that will deepen their capacity for intimacy, for love, and for compassion. However, this path is not for the faint of heart. It often requires going beyond the familiar comfort zones of self-protection and ego control. It requires equal amounts of courage and desire: to stand naked and vulnerable in front of our beloved; to see and be seen; to encounter one another beneath the level of opinions, assumptions, or narrow definitions we may have of ourselves or our partner. It requires an openness and a willingness to allow a radically different quality of experience to emerge; a deeper, freer, more essential experience of being in which we are able to truly behold and embrace our beloved partner, soul to soul. Some of our unquestioned assumptions about who we are, who our partner is, and what our relationship is—or needs to be—will undoubtedly require honest and humble reevaluation along the way. For it is almost certain that who we wake up to be will be far more than who we believed we were.

When a couple chooses to center and ground their relationship in the conscious intent to wake up, they are choosing a path that is extraordinarily rich, alive, and original; a path that will deepen their capacity for intimacy, for love, and for compassion.

But how do we go about waking up? How do we remove the veil of our ego trances and come to know ourselves and our partners as the spiritual beings we truly are? Waking up is not a single event, but an ongoing process. It can become a way life for those who choose to embark on the journey. It begins with a clear and genuine *intent* to live a more fully awake life, and a willingness to engage in a personalized practice of awakening that feels real and meaningful. Once we have developed a degree of mastery on our individual path, what we find is that there is a natural and easy shift and flow between the psychological and the spiritual aspects of ourselves that naturally extends to our relationships. Yet, these aspects must first be sorted out and clarified in order for us to fully experience, and benefit from, that natural and easy flow.

We are waking up from fear-based, suffering-filled, narrowly focused states of consciousness, which we will identify as avoidant or reactive trance states, or trances. We will, in chapter 2, examine different types of trance states and learn how we can be unwittingly trapped and defined by them. In later chapters, we will explore how trance states deeply affect the quality of our significant relationships.

This work is presented in two volumes. Volume One, which you hold in your hands, focuses primarily on the psychological realm to address what it is we are waking up *from*, and then develops a *practice of awakening* that expands from the individual into a dynamic interactive process for couples. Volume Two will address what it is we are waking up *into*, and will explore the spiritual, transpersonal, and transcendent aspects of who we are.

Together, we will embark on this journey, keeping a close eye on how we can approach our relationships as an ever deepening and expanding adventure of discovery, awe, and of love.

CHAPTER ONE 1

Cohesive Elements of a Relationship

Early on in my psychotherapy practice when I would interview a couple individually prior to meeting with them together, I would often be astounded at how different their descriptions were of the *same* relationship. There were times when, had I not known they were together, I would have thought they were describing completely different relationships. I would sometimes ask myself silently, "How in the world did these two ever get together?" or, "How do they stay together, they aren't even in the same relationship?"

I can now answer those questions. From three decades of observing and learning about couple relationships—my own as well as those I have worked with—I have found certain universal elements that consistently function as the glue which holds a couple together. I have distilled these into three essential categories that I refer to as the ***cohesive elements of a relationship***.

- A shared (or compatible) vision
- Intrinsically rewarding moments
- Complementary dysfunctional patterns

There is no particular order in which these elements occur in a relationship, as each is unique. Some relationships only have one of the elements, others two, and still other relationships contain all three. While the configuration and predominance of the elements may vary with different relationships and can shift within the same relationship, I have never known a couple to remain together when there was not at least one of these elements present.

A Shared (or Compatible) Vision

A vision is the picture that each of us holds of our place in the world, in our spiritual universe, in our relationships, or of our life's path. A vision is often a projection of some aspect of ourselves. It could also represent a sense of purpose or our reason for being. Sometimes this might get translated into a mission, such as feeding the starving children of third-world countries, or saving the rain forests, or becoming a political leader in order to make dramatic policy changes. But a vision does not have to be a mission at all, or to exist on such a grand scale. It could be something as basic as the desire to raise a family in a certain way, or to own a Mom and Pop's diner, or to renovate a farmhouse, or to live in the country. It could be adventurous or practical, serious or playful, earthy or materialistic or mythic.

While not all personal visions directly affect the couple relationship, there is usually some degree of overlap. For example, whether one envisions a career as a doctor or a farmer or writer or a restaurant owner may not be about the relationship, per se. But the lifestyle needed to support such a career is often crucial to its success. So, of particular importance here is the couple's shared vision of their relationship. Open and clear communication about this is extremely important. Yet, all too often, the vision either goes unexpressed, is taken for granted, or is not considered at all.

Sometimes a couple may think they have a shared vision when, in fact, they don't. For example, one person may assume that marriage implies a whole set of roles and expectations and not realize that their partner does not share the same assumptions. In fact, for their partner, marriage may imply quite a different set of roles and expectations. In effect, the marriage serves as an implicit contract, the terms of which each partner believes that the other is freely and happily agreeing to. Then, down the road, one person is likely to feel betrayed or cheated when the other does not live up to their end of the contract. The other person, operating from a different understanding of their agreement, may be quite dismayed when they find out that, according to their partner, they were doing something wrong. In fact, based on their own assumptions, that person may have a completely different perception of who is betraying whom!

What matters is not what the vision is, but that the two individuals share the same or, at the very least, compatible visions. And, in order to have a cohesive effect, this shared or compatible vision must be individually authentic. That is, it must be independently held and genuinely valued by each person, and must not be one person's accommodation or concession to their partner's vision in order to please (or keep) them. Conceding one's own true vision out of fear of losing a relationship is an act of codependency, and would not constitute a true sharing. Specific goals and plans could certainly be involved and may well need to be negotiated along the way. But the vision itself would reflect something essential and meaningful about each person and could not be significantly compromised without that person's integrity also being compromised.

This is not to say that a person's vision cannot change, or that he or she cannot develop a genuine vision that is in some way an outgrowth of the relationship. In fact, one of the unexpected gifts of a relationship is often the discovery or growth of some true aspect of self which was unrecognized or undeveloped before the relationship. Our visions will inevitably reflect aspects of ourselves of which we are aware, and so, as we live and grow in our self-awareness, so will our visions live and grow and change accordingly. In the following example, we will meet one of the couples we will visit from time to time who will help us to clarify how the ideas presented can actually play out in our relationships. Let us now see how a shared, or compatible, vision manifests in Jessie's and Patrick's relationship.

Jessie and Patrick met in their late thirties, both having been married once before. Jessie's marriage—in her mid-twenties—was ill-fated and short-lived. Patrick had been married for almost ten years to a woman who had two children from a prior marriage. She and Patrick had one daughter, Sara, who was four years old at the time of the divorce, and since then, has lived half the time with Patrick.

Patrick, a successful real estate broker and residential land developer had felt, for a number of years, like he was not doing what he was meant to do with his life. His career, in particular, lacked a depth of meaning and purpose that left him feeling "off course" in some way, and empty. When Jessie met Patrick, she was an assistant manager of a successful plant nursery, as well as a public speaker and educator on a variety of subjects, including horticulture, environmental awareness, organic gardening, and composting. They met at a conference on "Sustainable Living," where Patrick attended a workshop that Jessie presented.

Their first meeting led to a friendship that deepened over a period of several months and, ultimately, became romantic. As Patrick shared his continuing discontent with his career, Jessie revealed to him her personal longing for a deeper sense of community than she had been able to find in her current living situation. She had often dreamed of living in a community of kindred spirits who shared her love for the land and her desire to live in a respectful and harmonious relationship with the environment.

In time, a vision began to emerge which felt equally compelling to both Patrick and Jessie because it reflected what each of them valued individually, even though it was their relationship that served as the catalyst. This vision eventually became a project: the development of an eco-friendly, sustainable living, consciousness oriented, intentional community. This project served as a strong cohesive element in their relationship, creating a meaningful focus to Patrick's career while also fulfilling many of Jessie's deeply held desires and dreams.

Above is only one of an infinite number of ways a couple can share a vision. This book introduces another shared (or potentially shared) vision: the couple relationship as a spiritual path, and lays the foundation for an interactive practice of awakening. It is my hope that these ideas will stimulate and inspire those couples who feel a genuine resonance with them. But I would offer a word of caution for the first person of a relationship who happens to read this book. If you find value in it and want to share the book with your partner, by all means offer it to him or her. But please do not bully or badger them into accepting this as *their* vision. Like any other vision, to be genuinely shared and to have a cohesive effect on your relationship, it must ring true for each person, independent of what the other might want or need.

Intrinsically Rewarding Moments

This element refers to any shared experience that both partners of a couple would agree is, quite simply, its own reward. Such moments are generally present-oriented, without any particular agenda other than spontaneous enjoyment of the experience itself. It could be something as simple as spending Sunday mornings together, sipping coffee on the back porch and watching the birds. It could be a shared sense of humor. It could be erotic play or passionate lovemaking. It could be silently holding hands in bed in the middle of night listening to a thunderstorm. It could be reading a book together, or dining out, or growing a garden together, or traveling. It is an immersion in a moment that is mutually and intrinsically rewarding and therefore is experienced as complete unto itself.

An intrinsically rewarding moment can be as silly as making a ridiculous facial expression which causes you both to laugh, or as trivial as playing a favorite game of cards, or as profound as sharing the moment of your child's birth. Some moments can become ritualized over time and repetition, such as watching a favorite television show together every Thursday night, or taking the dog for a walk together every morning. Other moments may occur only once, but can be so exquisitely beautiful, or enchanted, or so meaningful in some way that they become a touchstone in a couple's life.

One night in late January, early on in their relationship, Patrick invited Jessie to his home for dinner. It was cold outside, so while a pot of chili was simmering on the stove, Jessie and Patrick sat in front of the fireplace and found themselves talking more deeply and intimately about their personal lives than they had before. Neither of them had heard the weather report earlier that day, which indicated the likelihood of a snowstorm. By the time the chili was ready and they were eating, the storm arrived in full force. They were having too much fun being together to cut their evening short, and agreed that Jessie could stay over in Sara's bedroom, since Sara was at her mother's.

It continued to snow heavily and, later in the evening, the power went out. Patrick lit a couple of oil lanterns and some candles, placing them around the room to augment the light from the fireplace. Patrick then remembered a rare bottle of whiskey a friend had given him. They opened the bottle, slipped off their shoes, and sat with their feet warming on the hearth. Their conversation moved so easily and naturally that they lost all track of time until very late in the night. At one point in a comfortable lull in the conversation, both noticed that the snowfall had stopped and the clouds had broken just enough to reveal a full moon, imbuing the evening with a surreal and magical quality. Everything was silent, the brilliant moonlight illuminated snow-covered tree limbs and nearby rooftops, and a soft white blanket of snow covered the ground.

It was that night that they made love for the first time. And, ever since that evening, snowstorms hold special meaning for them, and continue to be among their most treasured shared moments.

Of course, not everything we enjoy continues to sustain us over the course of a relationship. Circumstances, physical abilities, or natural developmental changes can shift our interests, our sensitivities, and our aesthetic preferences. Taking a twenty-mile backpacking trip into the wilderness may be an intrinsically rewarding experience for a couple at one point in their relationship, but may become not so rewarding if one or both of them becomes less physically able. Bird watching may simply be boring to a very young couple, but may become fascinating at another time in their lives. Children growing up and leaving home often opens up a whole new range of experiences for a couple. The ways in which a couple enjoys sex can also change as the relationship evolves and matures.

Times of deep personal upheaval, trauma, or catastrophe can also offer intrinsically rewarding moments, even though they may be less obvious at first. These can be precipitated by a major life event, such as a very serious illness or accident during which we may confront our own or our partner's death, a house fire, a flood that destroys cherished belongings, or a collective tragedy, such as war or a terrorist attack. All of these would force us to face and view life differently.

During extraordinary times such as these—when we are stripped of our normal comforts, routines, and expectations, when the solid ground of our ordinary existence has slipped out from under us—something quite remarkable can, and often does, occur. The sheer power and enormity of our experience is usually so overwhelming that sooner or later, it will exhaust us to the point of no longer being able to resist the full impact of our circumstances. We are then drawn down through layers of fear and pain and loss toward some deep interior well of feeling, some essential truth within ourselves, perhaps unknown until that moment. And, out of that descent, a recognition and appreciation of one another can emerge, so essential and so profound that it is felt to be nothing less than an encounter of souls.

Very few couples would knowingly choose devastating experiences. Yet many who do suffer through a shared ordeal report that while the experience was awful and something they would never choose to repeat, it was also one of the most transformative, beautiful lessons of love and growth and healing they have ever known.

Complementary Dysfunctional Patterns

People do not always stay together for emotionally healthy reasons. Here we encounter what we might call the complex psychological web of relationship. This is where the unhealed emotional wounds (and their associated ego defenses) of one person *commingles* with the unhealed emotional wounds (and defenses) of the other person to form a dysfunctional pattern of interaction within the relationship. More often than not, these defenses against emotional wounds form long before the current relationship ever begins, usually in childhood or adolescence. And what was perhaps a useful or necessary defense at that time gets generalized into a style of relating that tends to get reenacted throughout one's life until the wound is acknowledged and healed. If the particular style of one person's ego defenses happens to complement the other's style, a toxic bond will likely occur between them.

If the particular style of one person's ego defenses happens to complement the other's style, a toxic bond will likely occur between them.

For example, let's say you were the youngest child in a family of highly opinionated parents and siblings. Early on, when you expressed an opinion, you were teased by your brother or sister or parents for being silly, immature, or ignorant. Hurt from the perceived rejection, and hungry to be accepted, you discovered early on that when you placed yourself in an inquiring "student" role, you were enthusiastically received. Now your family members were pleased because they could satisfy their desire to express their ideas, and you found your place of belonging by listening. You were not being authentic and spontaneous in this role, because you did not feel safe. Instead, you were carefully avoiding the emotional vulnerability of feeling hurt and rejected. But the strategy worked, at least superficially. And because it worked, it became incorporated into a style of interaction that gets played out over and over again.

Now, let's suppose your current partner grew up in a family in which being timid or deferential was disapproved of. In that family, being smart, knowledgeable, and opinionated was rewarded. When they did not understand something or could not answer a questions posed to them, they felt shame and feared potential rejection. So, early on, they learned to express ideas and opinions as often as possible. The family was pleased and proud of their "little genius" and encouraged them to always pursue knowledge. Since this behavior assured your partner of the acceptance they clearly needed, it became incorporated into their style of interaction from then on.

In both your and your partner's case, these adaptive behaviors were the best you could come up with at the time they originated, given the limited resources and emotional development that you had to draw upon as children. Yet, while the behaviors served to keep you both "emotionally safe" as children, they become a significant hindrance to true intimacy in adult relationships. It is much like wearing a life jacket in the water. It will keep you safely afloat when you cannot swim. But, if you never take it off, it will greatly limit your *ability* to swim.

So now, we have two adaptive styles of interaction that are complementary. They function as counterparts to each other. A teacher needs a student in order to teach. A student needs a teacher to learn from and defer to. On the surface, it might appear that this couple is a match made in heaven. They both are secure in their respective roles. And this would be true if these styles of behavior were authentic responses of emotionally present, fully conscious adults. But, in fact, they are the fear-based adaptive behaviors of each child, unwittingly projected onto their adult relationship. They are not even about their actual current relationship. Just as in childhood, they are avoiding the vulnerability of true intimacy.

What makes any pattern of behavior dysfunctional is that: 1. it is based on a false premise about the present moment (though it may have had a historical validity); 2. personal awareness is significantly limited or distorted; and, 3. feelings, perceptions, and reactions occur automatically according to a pre-established pattern. What makes dysfunctional behaviors complementary is that they occur as paired bonds, such as in our teacher/student example. One behavior actually depends upon its complement in order to function as a cohesive element in the relationship.

There are all kinds of *complementary dysfunctional patterns* of behavior in couple relationships. While some of the more common ones include, abuser/victim; alcoholic/enabler; critical parent/defensive child; down trodden/rescuer; controller/placater, each couple creates their own unique combination or set of combinations.*

Quite often, when a couple seeks professional assistance, it is because there has been some change in the configuration of the cohesive elements that has disrupted (or is threatening to disrupt) the stability of the relationship. An element that was once prominent may begin to recede or, conversely, an element that did not seem to be present before might emerge. For instance, a couple may have entered into a new stage of life or of the relationship, such as getting married, having a child, buying a home together, moving to a new town, one or both retiring or changing a career, etc.

At some point, the pain and weariness may begin to outweigh the beauty and the joy.

What might have been a shared vision at one stage of the relationship may have run its course, or changed. Perhaps a latent or dormant dysfunctional pattern emerged in reaction to a developmental stage or life event; or perhaps there has been a cumulative effect of hurt, distrust, or resentment from a long-standing dysfunctional pattern that was never resolved. Over time, this may erode the openness or ability to enjoy the intrinsically rewarding moments that once fed the relationship. At some point, the pain and weariness may begin to outweigh the beauty and the joy.

Sometimes, what was once a complementary dysfunctional pattern will become obsolete, such as when one person heals, outgrows, or for whatever reason, disengages from their end of the pattern. If the other person does not "hook" the newly freed partner back into the pattern, the change will have a destabilizing effect on the relationship. Unsettling as this may feel,

*There have been a number of books written in the past two decades that examine in depth specific psychological patterns that reflect particular complementary dysfunctional patterns. Three classic works that come to mind are: *Co-Dependent No More* by Melody Beattie, *Women Who Love Too Much* by Robin Norwood, and *Emotional Blackmail* by Susan Forward.

it can be a couple's much needed "wake-up call" to heal the wounds which lie beneath the old pattern, and to revitalize their relationship.

However, if the prior dysfunctional pattern was their predominant (or only) cohesive element, the couple will find themselves in a serious crisis. Without significant growth by both, the relationship will not likely remain intact. Ironically, the healing and growth sometimes will reveal that, were it not for the complementary dysfunctional pattern, they would not have become a couple in the first place. Should they choose to remain together, independent of their old pattern, it would be as if they were creating an entirely new relationship.

***

The primary focus of Volume One of *Waking Up Together* is to provide a way for couples to free themselves from the pain and suffering of complementary dysfunctional patterns, and to discover the depths of love, joy, and fulfillment that come whenever we encounter the authentic spiritual beings that we truly are. To do this we must look deeper than the surface interactions where the ego dramas of our dysfunctional patterns play themselves out; ego dramas such as arguments or power struggles, betrayals, emotional reactivity, hurt feelings, painful misunderstandings, perpetual frustrations, and unmet needs. As consuming as these experiences can be, they are only the symptoms of underlying dysfunctional patterns. To become free from the painful dramas, we must understand the underlying patterns that create and sustain them. These patterns are the underpinnings, the structural foundation of our dysfunctional interactions. This is the level where true and lasting change can occur.

To become free from the painful dramas, we must understand the underlying patterns that create and sustain them.

In the following chapter we will examine the structural foundation of our dysfunctional patterns and come to understand how they occur in the first place. In doing this, we will learn how consciousness tends to organize itself into specific and discrete states of consciousness known as trances and how these trances become incorporated into our every-day, ordinary lives, usually without our even noticing them. In subsequent chapters we will explore how the propensity for entering trances extends into our relationships and, ultimately, how we can learn to wake up from them, first individually and then with our partner.

CHAPTER TWO

Trance Consciousness

Suppose you decide to go to the movie theater, looking forward to a pleasant evening of entertainment. Let's further imagine that you have heard of several good movies that are currently playing that you must choose between: an action film, a comedy, a romance movie, a thriller, a political drama, a science fiction movie, a light whimsical fantasy, and an intellectually complex foreign film with subtitles. How do you go about choosing? While most of us tend to gravitate toward our favorite genres, our final choice will usually be determined by the mood we are in, or the mood we hope the movie will put us in.

We generally go to a movie to be stimulated in some way: emotionally, intellectually, or sensually. We may hope to be moved, inspired, surprised, or perhaps just to be distracted from something unpleasant occurring in our personal life. Whatever the reason, movies that are the most successful are those which capture our interest and our attention so completely that, at least for certain moments, we become totally absorbed in the action, scenery, story, dialogue, and/or emotion. Our bodies may become engaged as well, with subtle changes in muscle tension or our breathing pattern. Caught up in the drama as if it was our own, we erupt with spontaneous laughter or tears. Depending on the type of movie or scene, our heart rate may increase, hormones may be released, we may jump or squirm in our seat, or blurt out a sound in surprise. In those moments, we even forget that we are watching a movie. In those moments, we are *entranced.*

One of the more impactful discoveries of both anthropology and psychology reveals for us the pervasiveness of the phenomenon of trance states in human consciousness. Indigenous cultures throughout history have incorporated the intentional application of hypnotic and other types of trance states into their spiritual and healing practices. Modern medicinal uses of hypnotic trance range from reducing stress and lowering heart rate and blood pressure, to reducing surgery recovery time, supporting immune system response, and more effectively managing acute and chronic pain. The therapeutic use of hypnotic trance in contemporary psychology, as well, has more than proven its effectiveness in areas such as addictions, therapeutic regression, accessing and healing trauma memories and other core issues trapped in the unconscious.

In addition to the intentional use of hypnotic trances, human consciousness seems to be exquisitely designed to be able to enter a variety of trance states spontaneously, which it does quite often. Some trances serve to enhance our ability to function effectively at a particular task or in certain situations, such as in a variety of athletic activities, artistic and musical performances, or certain mechanical operations where a sustained focus is required. On the other end of the spectrum, other trances may prove to be psychologically or interpersonally dysfunctional, even destructive. We are so naturalized to this process, we generally do not even notice when we have entered a trance state. Many of us are not aware that trance states of consciousness play an integral part of our everyday lives. Stephen Wolinsky, Ph.D., elucidates this phenomenon beautifully in his ground-breaking book *Trances People Live* (1991).

It is common to have our attention absorbed and captivated while watching a movie. That experience is obvious to even the casual observer and we don't generally give it a second thought. What most of us do not realize is that a very similar phenomenon occurs inside our own mind throughout the day, yet we are so conditioned to it that it blends unnoticed into our ordinary daily lives. It is as if we are going to the movies inside our own mind and get so caught up in the drama that we forget we are watching a movie. As we consider this analogy more carefully, we will shed more light on how trances operate in our everyday lives.

Think of the basic components that make up the movie experience. For our purposes we will simplify these into: filming, editing, projecting the film onto a screen, and, finally, the viewing. Central to this entire process, from the filming to the viewing, is the function of selectivity.

In a sense we could say the mind is constantly "filming" the ongoing circumstances, events, activities, and experiences of our lives as they occur. That is, we are continuously perceiving, processing, and recording these experiences, which include any feelings, thoughts, sensations, or interpretations that are part of the experience. Of course, how we process and record these experiences is neither random nor objective—but involves a highly selective "editing" process. The "scene" will always be shot from a uniquely personal perspective, and our "inner camera" will always have the "lens" and "filters" of our beliefs and assumptions, likes and dislikes, attitudes, feelings, needs, past experiences, and current expectations—all of which significantly influence the subjective nature and quality of our experiences. In addition to the lens and filters that shape and color our initial experience, we continue to edit and revise our memories as we delete, embellish, change our perspective, or ascribe new meaning to a past experience.

When we enter a new experience, the film is usually already running and gets "projected" onto the "screen" of whatever circumstance or event that is occurring, or onto the person we happen to be interacting with. And just like those moments in a movie theater, we become so absorbed by and identified with the drama, for the moment we don't realize that a movie is playing in our minds that we are projecting onto the situation. This is equally true whether our movie is pleasant or unpleasant, painful, or destructive.

Because we can so easily slip in and out of trances, often without realizing it, gaining a clear understanding of the differences between a fully awake state and a trance state will help us to be more aware of those shifts of consciousness when they occur. As stated in the introduction, Volume Two of *Waking Up Together* will be devoted to exploring the depths and parameters of a life path of spiritual awakening with the emphasis on what we are waking up *into*. But for the immediate purpose of contrast, there are a few basic characteristics of an awake state that we can identify.

An awake state, in this context, refers to both the content and the quality of one's consciousness. First of all, full present awareness means being alert to, and fully conscious of, what is occurring in the present moment. This includes not only what is occurring externally in our immediate environment, but also what is occurring within us, such as our own thoughts and impressions, and the full range of our emotional and physical feelings and sensations.

How we perceive what is taking place within us and around us from an awake state will most likely be quite different than perceptions that arise from our conditioned mental biases. There is a kind of perceptual innocence that characterizes an awake state. What we perceive is not distorted, obscured, defined, or judged by preconceived beliefs, or interpretations, or categorizations. We could say there is a natural and inherent "Zen-like" quality that characterizes an awake state of consciousness.

When we are fully awake, the present moment is experienced as having its own intrinsic value, rather than merely being a bridge to the next thing, the next event, or task or project we might be anticipating. Being awake in the moment does not possess a future-oriented momentum and thereby fosters a mental quality of stillness and quiet that, in turn, allows our consciousness to deepen and expand. We are able to fully perceive and interact with what is before us without the compulsion to be emotionally reactive or the need to change what we are experiencing. The general quality of our heart and mind will be peaceful, open, receptive, and humble.

Being awake in the moment fosters a mental quality of stillness and quiet that, in turn, allows our consciousness to deepen and expand.

A number of spiritual teachers have emphasized this quality of full present awareness as central to their teachings. J. Krishnamurti, one of the great spiritual teachers of the twentieth century, spent the better part of his life speaking and writing about the shift or opening into this dimension of consciousness, which he focused on in several of his books, including *The Only Revolution* (1970), and *The Awakening of Intelligence* (1973). There are also several contemporary teachers who address much the same thing, such as Eckhart Tolle, who beautifully articulates this quality of presence in his books, *The Power of Now* (1999), and *A New Earth* (2005). Gangaji also addresses this shift in awareness as "discovering the truth of who you are" in her book, *The Diamond in Your Pocket* (2005).

As we examine the nature and quality of trance consciousness throughout this chapter, the differences between an awake state and a trance state will become increasingly clear. Let us begin with a basic definition and description of a hypnotic trance that we will build upon as we continue.

A trance state, for our purposes, can be defined as "a specialized state of consciousness that is characterized by the withdrawal of one's attention from full present awareness, and a simultaneous redirection and fixation of attention to a narrow pattern of perception, feeling, and sensation; often—but not always—giving the impression of "going deeply within" one's own inner experience."

A hypnotic trance can be most easily understood as having two essential components that occur simultaneously:

1. a contraction (or shrinking) of full present awareness into a narrowly focused state, or channel, of consciousness, and,
2. a personal identification or fusion with that state (as if you were "entering into" it) to the extent that it determines the nature and quality of your subjective experience for as long as you are in it.

Each of us has a natural propensity for entering trances that we inadvertently bring to our intimate relationships. Very often, the unrecognized trances of each individual become so entwined in their interactions with each other, that entire "pockets" of the relationship occur in one trance state or another. The extent to which a couple is operating entranced, as well as the types of trances entered, depends on how psychologically present and aware each person is. For some, the couple relationship, itself is, by and large, a shared trance.

Six Characteristics of Trance States

This section more fully describes six common characteristics of trance states and offers examples that will be helpful to understand as we begin to explore how the trance phenomenon impacts our relationships.

1. A trance state generally manifests as a specific and discrete pattern of consciousness that acts as a temporary filter or lens of perception. Thoughts, feelings, events and sensory data are all selected, edited, interpreted, and categorized in order to be congruent with the particular lens through which we are perceiving our environment. Because of this, trance realities tend to be self-confirming, even when full present awareness would likely elicit a markedly different perception. For example, let's suppose that one partner comes home with a new hairstyle, hoping that her mate will like the new look. Two days later, hurt and irritated, she finally blurts out, "You hate it!"

"Hate what?" her partner may respond innocently, though with a tinge of trepidation.

"I know you hate my hair. I had it cut two days ago and you haven't said a thing."

Staring mutely, he notices her new hairstyle for the first time, even though he had looked at her many times since it had been cut. His particular trance involved seeing her through the lens of his mental image of her, which edited out information that did not conform to the image he held in his mind. She interrupted his trance simply by bringing his attention to the actual moment they were in. Then, he was able to see the obvious.

2. While fully immersed in a trance state, we only have access to the resources—knowledge, skills, choices, perceptions, emotional repertoire—that are part of the trance state itself. It is much like opening a computer file. Once opened, we have access to all the information stored within that file. Our hard drive has other capabilities, including access to other sources of information or files, but as long as we are in a particular file, we are limited to the functions and information contained in that file.

A phenomenon known as state-bound learning and memory comes into play here. This refers to a natural tendency for any particular set of knowledge or skills, or unique experience to become initially associated with, or bound to, the state of consciousness we were in when we originally learned the knowledge or skill, or had the experience. Once we learn something while in a particular state, it will be much easier to access or retrieve that knowledge, skill, or experience at a later time when we re-enter the original state of consciousness in which the learning took place.*

Think of the college student who takes speed all weekend to stay awake in order to cram for a Monday morning exam. Having been awake all night on speed, he is still in a bit of an altered state of consciousness when he takes the exam. Because of the neurological link between the speed-induced state and the material studied, he is able to remember most of what he learned and passes the test quite easily. A few days later, when he is in his ordinary state, he can't remember nearly as much. Yet, if he takes more speed, lo and behold, he now remembers the material!

The following experiment is one I remember hearing about several years ago regarding state-bound learning and memory. While unorthodox, and not a practice I would condone under ordinary circumstances, this experiment helps to highlight the striking and compelling link between the state we are in while learning, and our ability to recall the state under similar conditions at a later time.

> Researchers divided college students who were entering a driving instruction course into two groups, being careful to make sure the two groups were demographically equal in terms of age, sex, race, etc. Both groups had the same instructor, followed identical course material, and met on alternate evenings each week until the course was completed.
>
> Immediately preceding each class, every student in the experimental group was served two to three alcoholic drinks, an amount sufficient to produce a moderate degree of intoxication. The researchers varied the number of drinks in order to approximate the same blood alcohol level in each of the subjects. No one in the control group drank any alcohol before or during class.
>
> At the end of the course, both groups took two final driving skills tests that included turning, parallel parking, stopping on a mark, and weaving between cones in a parking lot in a timed test. The examiners deducted points for mistakes or misjudgments of distance or space, or slowed response time. Immediately preceding the first test, all students in both groups were served

---

*Ernest Rossi devotes an entire chapter (3) to this phenomenon in his book *The Pyschobiology Of Mind-Body Healing: New Concepts of Therapeutic Hypnosis* (1986).

two to three alcoholic drinks. For the second test, no alcohol was consumed by either group prior to the driving test. This created four categories of drivers, those who:

a. learned to drive while sober, and were tested while sober
b. learned to drive while sober, and were tested while intoxicated
c. learned to drive while intoxicated, and were tested while sober
d. learned to drive while intoxicated, and were tested while intoxicated

The test results were ranked in four categories:

1. the best drivers (meaning the fewest mistakes within the given time limits)
2. the second best drivers
3. the third best drivers
4. the worst drivers (meaning the most mistakes within the given time limits)

The test results revealed an interesting pattern: the best drivers (1) and the second best drivers (2) were very closely matched in skill. But there was a significant drop of skill in the third best drivers (3) and the worst drivers (4), who were also closely matched to each other. When the researchers matched the categories of students with the test results, something quite interesting was revealed. To no one's surprise, the best driving results were obtained by those who learned to drive while sober and were tested while sober. Yet the results were almost as high for those who learned to drive while intoxicated and were tested while intoxicated. There was a significant drop in test results for those who learned to drive while intoxicated and were tested while sober. And slightly worse results from those who learned to drive while sober and were tested while intoxicated.

It is very unfortunate that most people who drive while intoxicated learned to drive while sober, which places them in the very worst category of driving skills!

State-bound learning and memory explains why the groupings of (a.) and (b.) categories had the best results. Those drivers were in the same state when they were tested as when they learned to drive. The significant drop in the skill level of (c.) and (d.) results is explained conversely. Both groups were in a different state when tested than they were when learning to drive. Access to the learned skill, including sensory and kinesthetic memory, was more difficult to attain. It is likely that those who were tested sober and did slightly better than those who were tested while intoxicated were better equipped to adjust and compensate for confusion and for unknowns and/or limited skill or knowledge.

3. Once a trance is engaged, it tends to remain intact until it runs its full course or is interrupted. For example, have you ever been driving while having an animated conversation with someone, or were deep in thought? When you arrived at your destination and turned off the ignition, you seemed to "come to" and could hardly remember the drive at all. In fact, it felt as if you weren't even the one driving! Yet, hundreds of minute observations, judgments, and decisions occurred in the course of the drive. Part of your mind was operating in a "driving trance," slightly outside your conscious attention, while the rest of your mind was engaged in the conversation or train of thought. The trance ended naturally when you arrived, allowing you to have full present awareness. But had a car or dog or person suddenly entered your path, the interruption would have immediately snapped you out of your driving trance, allowing you to be fully present to respond to the emergency situation.

4. A trance that holds emotional significance for an individual, and recurs many times, will develop its own familiar content, rhythm, texture and feeling tone, all of which is reactivated every time the trance is engaged. The subjective experience that is created and uniquely attuned to a particular state tends to solidify, through time and repetition, into a specialized experience of self generally referred to as a *trance identity*. Entering a trance becomes synonymous with taking on, or fusing with, that identity.

5. Once a trance pattern has been established, it may temporarily recede from our conscious awareness into a relatively dormant or inactive state. A trance pattern is comprised of a variety of intricately associated elements of an experience. These elements could include the situation or event, any thoughts, emotions, or interactions that accompanied the experience, and any related physical movements, sensations, sights, sounds, or smells that may have been part of the total experience. Any single element or combination of elements experienced at another time could activate or trigger—by association—the re-emergence of the entire trance experience. Hearing a song that you shared with a partner may reactivate a momentary reliving of that relationship, stirring up familiar sensations and rekindling old feelings.

Finding a picture of a beloved pet that died years ago could reawaken a whole spectrum of experience, from tenderness and beauty or humor, to any aspects of grief that may not be fully healed. Unexpectedly bumping into someone from a past relationship that ended in hurt and bitterness may stimulate a very unpleasant contracted trance experience that feels as awful and destructive as it did when it happened. Experiencing a particular type of sexual encounter may activate the reliving of a similar prior sexual experience that may have been painful or even traumatic. In these examples, the activation of a current sensation can be directly linked with the trigger. However, many trance patterns can be activated with no conscious, or easily recognizable awareness of the original cause or trigger.

6. Because a trance state is a contraction of consciousness away from full present awareness, we no longer have full present awareness as an immediate basis for contrast and perspective. Therefore, while we are in a hypnotic trance, we generally will not realize it. In retrospect, we may well recognize the trance we were in. But while in the trance, it was the only reality we were aware of.

Because some common aspects of consciousness can occur in both awake and trance states, such as association and memory, the distinction between those states might seem a bit ambiguous at first. Yet, knowing the difference between an awake response to a given situation and a trance reaction is significant and important. To help clarify the difference, the following example begins by presenting an emotional historical context for a painful and debilitating reactive trance. This will be followed by a present-time situation that could be a typical trigger for such a trance, and then we will consider the difference between the trance reaction and an awake response.

When Hilary was in middle school, her father struggled with mild chronic depression, and a deep and largely unexamined rage that he told himself was related to work and which he suppressed with only moderate success. Despite his inner struggles, he loved Hilary and was generally kind and amiable toward her, to which she eagerly responded with much affection.

However, about once a month, usually on a Friday evening on his way home from work, Hilary's father would buy a bottle of bourbon and consume most of it over the course of the evening. It was on these evenings that his rage would begin to emerge. After the first couple of drinks, he seemed relaxed, but as the night progressed he would become irritable, and then argumentative, and sometimes openly hostile. Hilary was confused and dismayed by this "change of personality." Sometimes she would try to shrug it off, but at other times, she would stand her ground and argue back with her father. On one occasion, with tempers flaring, she pushed harder than usual, challenging his behavior, and accused him of being mean and stupid. In a burst of anger, he slapped her in the face hard enough to knock her backwards, sending her sprawling to the floor.

While Hilary was not injured physically, she was heartbroken. Her father was devastated by his behavior. With deep feelings of remorse, he promised never to hit her again; a promise that he faithfully kept. Hilary forgave him because she loved him, but never fully trusted him again, especially when he drank bourbon. Much of her innocence was lost because of that experience, and the foundation of her usual self-confidence and sense of personal safety was compromised for years to come. On future occasions, when her father came home smelling of bourbon, she found excuses to leave the house or to stay in her bedroom, trying to distract herself from the nagging anxiety in the pit of her stomach.

In time, her father received the help he needed, addressing the issues that lay beneath his anger and depression, and stopped abusing alcohol. Hilary managed to compartmentalize her wound, and continued her life in an overtly normal and productive way. By the time she was thirty-two, Hilary was a physically healthy and vigorous single woman with an active social life. She was also a very competent and talented administrative assistant in a locally owned business. She had risen to that position partly because she was an excellent manager of people, but also because of her ability to assess problems early on and to solve them in creative and resourceful ways. Robert, her boss, didn't have the best communication skills, but was smart and generally fair-minded when it came to dealing with his employees.

On one particular Friday afternoon, however, Hilary stayed later than the other employees because she needed to finish a report. Robert's behavior had been odd that day. After returning from a lunch meeting, he isolated himself in his office and refused to take any calls or speak to anyone. About a half hour after everyone else had left, he came out of his office and entered Hilary's, agitated and distracted. He began to rant about something that had happened earlier that day, but was not very rational in the way he was expressing himself. When Hilary questioned what he was saying, he reacted with an uncharacteristic outburst of anger, which startled her. It was when he leaned forward, close to her face, that Hilary noticed the distinct smell of bourbon on his breath.

> In an awake state, while she may be informed by her past experience, she will not be defined by it.

At this point, Hilary is at a critical moment. If she has not truly healed her wounds related to her father's abusive drinking and violence (emotional as well as physical), the entire complex of her experience with her father will likely have remained compartmentalized and submerged in its original pattern. Although it may plague her in subtle and toxic ways generally, it may not emerge consciously in full force until and unless it is triggered by some later event or situation. Any of the elements of this situation could serve as a trigger. The fact that it is Friday afternoon and she is alone with a male authority figure could be a triggering element. The intensity of Robert's anger—particularly its unexpected volatility—or the smell of bourbon on his breath could trigger her trance. The combination of these elements could create an especially powerful trigger to activate the entire compartmentalized trance of her adolescent terror, hurt, and powerlessness.

If this encounter triggers a trance, it is not that Hilary will simply remember how it was when she was in middle school. She will feel twelve years old again. She will feel frightened, powerless, and hurt as if she was reliving her original traumatic experience. She will not have access to the knowledge, wisdom, or perspective of a fully present and empowered adult woman. She could find herself recoiling physically, or crying. She could experience other sensations or images she had forgotten about but which were part of her adolescent experience. She likely will feel victimized and unsafe, just as she once felt as a child. And, in a trance, she would not question her emotional response or present "reality."

However, if Hilary has, at least to some extent, healed the wounds of her past, she more likely will remain fully present and awake. She will have access to all of the wisdom of her life experience as a capable adult woman. She will be able to utilize her ability to assess problems and come up with creative solutions, and apply her finely honed interpersonal skills—all of which have placed her in the job in which she currently excels. Her lack of emotional reactivity will allow Hilary to not take her boss's behavior personally. Rather, from her awake and present adult perspective, she will be able to clearly recognize the inappropriate—and out of character—behavior of her boss, ascertain the distinct likelihood that he is in some kind of pain or duress, accurately determine the uselessness of arguing with or challenging him while he is drunk, and manage him in a skillful and compassionate way. If he continues to be unresponsive, or is in any way abusive, she will simply leave.

With full present awareness, this situation may stimulate a surge of memories, from the smell of bourbon to the aggressive behavior, not to mention old emotional pain. Hilary might well be struck by the similarity between Robert's behavior and her father's in the past. But she will not confuse the past with the present. In an awake state, while she may be informed by her past experience, she will not be defined by it.

When we are in full present awareness, two things occur. First, our experience is not filtered through past experiences, definitions, or cultural or societal constraints. Each moment presents itself as a new, fresh, innocent awareness. Therefore, all of our responses will be oriented to what is occurring in present time, with no historical baggage or assumptions. Second, we will be free to experience the moment as original, and our responses will be spontaneous and present-oriented.

Six Contexts of Trances

It is important to keep in mind that hypnotic trances are not "good" or "bad," in and of themselves; we all have the capacity to enter trance states. This inherent ability is natural and can be very beneficial at times. Whether a particular trance is experienced as positive or negative, healthy or unhealthy, depends upon the content and context in which it occurs. Following are six common contexts out of which a trance state can emerge.

1. Neutral or passive

The passive reverie of deep relaxation, fatigue, or a leisure activity. This could include daydreaming, reading a novel, watching a movie or TV show, or any other similar passive activity in which we are so absorbed that we become temporarily unaware of our immediate present circumstance and, so engaged, personally identify with its character(s), storyline, or energy. When we are deeply relaxed, we experience physiological and chemical changes—slowed breathing and heart rate, release of serotonin and other hormones—that are conducive to entering certain types of trance. Sitting by a pond on a lazy afternoon, becoming fascinated by a bathing duck, being mesmerized by the activity of a water spider, or becoming captivated by an unusual movement just below the surface of the pond—any of these activities could induce a light trance. The word "mesmerize" was derived from the name of Anton Mesmer, often considered the "father" of modern hypnosis.

2. "In the zone"

The act of engaging in an activity, skill, or behavior that is already linked to a specific and specialized state of consciousness, such as driving a car, playing a sport, playing a musical instrument, writing a novel, deciphering a mathematical puzzle, painting, or sculpting a work of art. This context applies particularly to experiences of creative and/or active or engagement in which we become truly engrossed. For most, the skill or activity was learned in a certain state of consciousness, and is most easily retrieved by reentering that same state. The state of consciousness and the associated activity are so inextricably linked that the activity automatically induces the state, which in turn, supports and facilitates the activity. This is referred to in sports as "being in the zone."

The state of awareness we observe in the Olympic diver just before she dives is not simply the mental concentration needed in order to remember all of the fine points of the dive. Ideally, she is putting herself in a deeply focused trance in which her intent, her vision of the dive, and her kinesthetic awareness are all intrinsically aligned with her *true* dive, while simultaneously screening out any distractions. This reminds me of a scene from the movie *The Legend of Bagger Vance* where the caddy, Bagger Vance, conveys this idea as he teaches a young boy to find his own "true authentic swing." This is similar to the artist who is so engrossed in his painting trance—where his grasp of color, form and light is inherent—that he may paint continuously for a full day, not even noticing that he missed two meals. Or the novelist who is so deeply engaged with the world she is creating on the page that she does not hear the phone ringing in the next room.

3. Sacred and intentional

The intentional use of trance in order to access specialized knowledge, information, or non-ordinary realms of consciousness for spiritual, visionary, or healing purposes. Unlike the other contexts, this involves a fully present and conscious choice to explore or examine aspects or realms of being that are generally not available in our ordinary daily routines and activities. In this context, the concentrated focus of a trance is used to penetrate the surface of ordinary consciousness in order to radically shift and expand our perspective.

The use of this type of trance has been acknowledged as part of sacred traditions as far back as human history has been recorded. Ideally, the experience is grounded in considerable knowledge, skill, self-awareness, and personal mastery. The entry into such a trance, alone or as a shared experience, is often ritualized and is preceded by a period of preparation and clarification of intent. Practices which are designed to help one access these types of trance states include chanting, trance dancing, sweat lodges, shamanic journeying, or other variations of soul travel, the use of psychoactive or spirit plants, certain types of meditative practice, fasting, or deep periods of extended prayer or solitude—especially in the wilderness, as in a vision quest. Paradoxically, the narrowed focus of sacred trance often becomes a portal into a greatly expanded experience of who we are.

4. *In our dreams*

The dreams of our sleep. Most people do not think of their nighttime dreams as being a trance state. Yet, a sleeping dream conforms to all the characteristics of a trance. A dream is simply a trance we are fully engaged in while physically asleep. It may seem more visually and experientially distinct from our waking life than other types of trances, but this is simply because in sleep, the withdrawal from our external reality is more perceptually distinct.

5. *Physical Ordeal or Trauma*

A reaction to acute, extreme, physical stress or trauma. This context refers to extreme physical situations that cause or induce a trance. Examples of such extreme physical situations include a serious injury, extremely intense physical pain, the ordeal of a prolonged childbirth, the onset of a high fever, various forms of physical torture, prolonged exposure to extreme weather conditions, or starvation. Trances brought on by such physical conditions tend to emerge in one of two ways. One way could be characterized as a dissociative or semiconscious state, such as when one is in shock. The other way has a more delirious or hallucinatory aspect, as can occur with a high fever or extreme sleep deprivation. If a physical ordeal also causes emotional trauma, that aspect could emerge later as an emotional avoidant or reactive trance.

> Many common psychological disorders can be understood as being part of, or nested within, one of many possible trance states.

6. *Emotional Avoidant or Reactive*

The escape from, or avoidance of, an emotional reality that is too painful, threatening, or overwhelming. The intent of trance in this context is to preserve a sense of safety and well-being by dissociating from what is perceived (or assumed) to be the source of harm.

Unfortunately, many of the problematic avoidant trances we enter in our adult lives unconsciously—seemingly without invitation—originated early in life, when we were subjected to circumstances that were too overwhelming for us to adequately manage or integrate. If, as a child, we were a victim of emotional, sexual, or physical abuse or neglect, or witnessed violence or some horrific or catastrophic event—any of these could be a powerful catalyst and cause for us as children to dissociate from full present awareness and to enter a trance state that would redirect our consciousness to a safer focus. But any number of less overtly traumatic social and emotional assaults of fear, shame, or hurt could also provide a powerful impetus for a trance reaction.

Such a trance might have served as a necessary defense mechanism for the child who did not yet have the emotional security, knowledge, or personal power to protect himself in other ways. So, as children, we learned to perceive cues that alerted us to immediate danger, cues that would become automatic triggers for entering a protective trance. Later, in adulthood, most of those cues still operate, and we are triggered into one or another of our avoidant trance states, even before we realize it. For instance, entering an age-regressed trance identity (sometimes referred to as our frightened, powerless, or wounded "inner child") operates more like a knee-jerk reaction than as a conscious choice.*

Many common psychological disorders can be understood as being part of, or nested within, one of many possible trance states. Whenever we react to emotional or physical pain or threat by automatically shifting into a less present state of consciousness, we have entered an avoidant trance. Such a trance will usually be characterized by a specific and consistent pattern of thoughts, perceptions, emotional reactions, and behaviors that seem to operate on their own, much like autopilot. The physical, emotional, and mental perceptual landscape of such a trance is frozen in time and remains unchanged. So, no matter how long ago we adopted a particular avoidant trance state, it will feel and look the same each and every time we enter it.

Often, there will also be some degree of physiological re-stimulation and/or a full sensory experience of the original occurrence, as if our body is re-living its original internal experience. This is sometimes referred to as cellular memory, and can be quite pronounced in extreme cases, such as with post-traumatic stress. For example, a number of my psychotherapy clients have reported that when they first begin to recall physical, sexual, or emotional abuse, their body goes into a hyper-excited state of alarm. They sometimes feel pain or contraction or numbness in the area or part of their body that experienced the brunt of their assault, as though the abuse was actually happening to them again, in the present moment even though, in the physical reality of my office, they are safe and unharmed.

---

*Wolinsky examines this particular type of trance in great depth in his book *The Dark Side Of The Inner Child* (1993).

Trances that are chosen freely, happily, and with conscious intent are, with few exceptions, highly beneficial and emotionally desirable. It is the trances that are triggered automatically and that trap us in a spiritually diminished, perceptually distorted, and emotionally reactive state that are problematic, both individually and in relationships. The greater the frequency or duration of time we stay in such a trance, the greater the negative influence it will have on our outlook on life and on how we relate to our partner. A long-standing trance, or one that is activated often, can easily become mis-identified as our personality. We may judge someone as grouchy or moody, insecure or jealous, lazy or irresponsible, anxious or neurotic. But such qualities do not accurately represent who that person is so much as they characterize the trances that he or she frequents.

While the first four contexts of trances are generally conducive to our mental, emotional, and spiritual well-being, we will focus most of our attention on the last context: the emotional avoidant or reactive trance. Emotional avoidant or reactive trances represent the unresolved issues or unhealed emotional wounds we've accumulated throughout our life that intrude upon and—all too often—dominate our present life and relationships. These trances are generally fear-based and are characterized by suffering of some kind. Having become habitualized over time, they never lead to real insight or growth, but simply reenact and repeat themselves blindly and automatically.

These are the trances that are of particular concern for a couple choosing to wake up together because they represent the core, the foundation of our complementary dysfunctional patterns. As illustrated in our example in chapter one, it is the particular quality and style of each person's avoidant or reactive trance that finds its complement in that of their partner's. If our avoidant or reactive trances are ignored and allowed to remain in operation beneath our conscious awareness, they will continue to undermine, erode, and severely limit the health and vitality of our significant relationships.

CHAPTER THREE

The Entranced Relationship

Most couples in the throes of a complementary dysfunctional pattern find themselves recycling the same issues, the same complaints, the same behaviors and interactions, and the same emotional reactions over and over. Frustrated and dismayed that no matter what they try to do in the hopes of changing their situation, they find themselves re-engaging in the same painful drama yet again.

One observation I have made regarding couples who argue often is that they do not have many different arguments. Rather, they usually have only one or two basic arguments that they simply rehash over and over. And, in these arguments, the couple's interactive pattern is so well established and habitual they could go on stage before an audience, each able to recite the entire script. They know how it begins, who says what, who challenges and who defends, how and when the emotional intensity ebbs and flows and builds, and who expresses which emotions. They both know which retort comes from whom and when it is most effective, where the argument crescendos, and how the whole interaction ends. Every now and then, someone might improvise and throw the other a curve, but even this is usually quickly incorporated into their dysfunctional pattern.

As emotionally painful and unrewarding as most complementary dysfunctional patterns are, they can be extremely tenacious. Even though a couple might learn to maneuver around the more painful aspects of their patterns, they often feel at a loss for how to truly end them. I have found this to be true because the couple focuses almost exclusively on the contents of the interactions. They keep re-addressing their particular issues, needs, positions, and reactive feelings as well as those of their partner, futilely attempting to create change or achieve some kind of resolution or agreement on that level. What they generally do not realize is that their dysfunctional patterns occur in, and are maintained within, specific states of consciousness, which we now recognize as trances.

> **Their dysfunctional patterns occur in, and are maintained within, specific states of consciousness.**

Complementary dysfunctional patterns represent avoidant trances that are engaged in by both partners of a relationship, simultaneously and interactively. Such a trance entered into by both partners serves as a kind of implicit agreement about their shared reality, which tends to be self-reinforcing. The more time both partners stay entranced, the greater the influence their trance has to shape the mood, the style, and the dynamics of the relationship. Often, a relationship unwittingly becomes habituated to a mixture of trance qualities, perceptions, and behaviors of the individual partners. The examples of complementary dysfunctional patterns named in the first chapter are relatively easy to identify because of the wide-spread media attention given to them in recent years. But subtler, less pronounced, and harder-to-identify, dysfunctional trances are also prevalent.

The term "entranced relationship" is used in a fluid—rather than a static—sense. It refers to both the individual and the shared trance states present in a relationship in any given moment. An individual or a couple usually becomes entranced periodically or situationally, but does not remain entranced all the time. The following example illustrates one way a couple might function while entranced without even realizing it.

Janet and William are in their mid-30s and have been married for seven years. They were both physically active and in good shape when they first met. Over the past couple of years, while William has put on a few extra pounds and has begun to lose some of his hair, Janet has continued to work out regularly and has remained very physically fit. Janet has always been the more social and gregarious of the two and has been their primary social initiator with other couples. She is more interested in emotional and aesthetic matters than intellectual ideas. She is also bright and creative, and these qualities serve her well in her interior design consulting business. William has never been particularly comfortable dealing with intimate emotional matters, although he has always been helpful as a problem solver. His Ph.D. in chemistry led to a respectable job with a soft drink company as a quality control manager, where his problem-solving skills are highly sought after.

Janet and William genuinely love each other, but because their needs are so different, much of what they do for pleasure or renewal they tend to do independent of one another. William, who is rather shy and more introverted than Janet, finds refuge and renewal in doing yard work or hanging out in his workshop building things, such as bird houses and outdoor furniture, as well as doing minor carpentry repairs around the house. Janet would rather go to art galleries, cocktail parties, and conventions related to her career. One thing they do share is a mutual love for their two Boston Terriers, which they take for walks together most evenings after work.

William's company was planning a large Christmas party that William felt obligated to attend, but was not looking forward to. Janet, on the other hand, was excited about getting dressed up and having a fun evening out with William. She had picked out a particularly lovely black, low-cut dress that she hoped William would find as sexy to look at as she felt wearing it. She decided to wear her hair up, which would expose her neck and highlight the opal necklace and matching earrings William had given her on their fifth anniversary. The outfit worked. William found her stunningly beautiful and was warming up to the idea of going to the party. His excitement for Janet was offset, though, by feeling "dumpy," and by his anticipation of having to endure awkward social interactions. Once they arrived at the party, they gravitated toward the bar to "oil the social mechanism," as William was fond of saying.

For about the first hour and a half, Janet and William stayed together, chatting with other folks and having a few more drinks. Eventually, they joined one of William's work buddies who was sitting at a large table by himself. About that time, the dance band began playing. Janet loved to dance but rarely could get William to dance with her because he felt awkward and self-conscious. She persuaded him to dance once, but after that, no amount of pleading, teasing or seducing could entice him into a second one. Janet, pumped and ready to let loose, asked William if he minded if she found other dance partners. Relieved, he agreed instantly, but noticed that he felt a little anxious. William resumed a conversation with his friend, and Janet went to freshen her drink and scout around for a friendly face and dance partner.

About a half hour later, William heard Janet's laughter across the dance floor. Following the sound, he found her dancing with Keven Jameson, one of the shift supervisors who was single, very good looking, and had a reputation as a flirt. What William did not know until this moment as he watched Keven, was that he was a very good dancer. Was this swing or salsa? William wasn't sure, but it looked sexy and Keven seemed quite in command, and Janet was responding with obvious delight. In fact, Janet seemed giddy with pleasure, which pained William as he watched her dance. He felt his stomach tighten and his mouth go dry.

William tried to push his discomfort aside and refocus on his conversation with his friend, chiding himself for being so insecure. But after two more dances, he was almost beside himself. When Janet finally returned to their table, flushed and moist with sweat, it took a considerable act of self-discipline for William not to vent his feelings on her. But he didn't have to. His stiff body language and the icy look in his eyes made it very clear that he was not pleased. William's jealousy had been a sore spot between them in the past but never seemed serious enough to cause a real problem. Because of this, and because another couple had joined William and his friend while Janet was on the dance floor, she tried to dismiss William's mood and engage in the table conversation. But when Keven approached their table a little later, greeting everyone and asking Janet to dance again, Janet turned him down. She wanted to dance some more but felt like she couldn't, given how

William was reacting. But she was pissed. They remained at the party for a little longer, yet hardly speaking to each another.

It was William who spoke first as they were driving home. "You sure were having a good time on the dance floor tonight."

Janet had felt "edgy" before, when William acted jealous, but usually managed to respond with compassion and reassurance. Tonight, however, she was still a little tipsy from the drinking and had less skill in handling complicated emotional matters. Not only that, she was feeling cheated out of her fun and, at the same time, defensive about her behavior. So, at that moment, she had no patience for what she considered to be William's pettiness. Initially, she didn't speak.

"So, aren't you going to say anything?" William prodded.

"What do you want me to say?" Janet answered, coldly.

"Well, for starters, you could ask me if I had a good time tonight."

"I already know you didn't. You made that quite clear at the table."

"You sound mad."

Janet glared at him without speaking. She wasn't just angry. To her own surprise, she was getting madder and madder by the minute.

"You're mad at me because I didn't have a good time?" he challenged.

"Of course not, William. I'm mad at you because you couldn't let me have a good time. You were sour about going in the first place. I dressed up for you but that wasn't enough. I tried to get you to dance with me. But you acted like you were doing me a favor rather than wanting to be with me."

"That's not true," he quickly responded.

"Like hell it's not. And you only danced once. Even though I practically begged you. But no. So I decided I wasn't going to let you spoil my evening just because you were a stick in the mud. Which I did by finding somebody else to dance with. But you had to punish me for that, too."

"I wasn't punishing you, Janet."

"Bullshit. Are you telling me that cold scowling look when I came back to the table wasn't to punish me?"

"I was just upset."

"Upset? About what?" she asked.

"You know damn well about what. Keven Jameson is a flirt and you were eating it up!"

"I was just having fun with someone who wanted to have fun, too. It's not my fault you chose to sit on your ass all night. I didn't do anything wrong."

"Janet, how could you think it would be okay for you to gush all over another man?"

"I wasn't gushing. William, I have never betrayed you, and I've had plenty of opportunities. I resent the hell out of your implication."

"Oh, you've had opportunities? Like, when?"

Clearly, this fight could continue indefinitely. And, the longer they argue, the nastier and more hurtful it will likely become. To put this in context of trance states, William began the evening already entranced. His long-standing feelings of low self-esteem and inadequacy had become a facet of his ego identity, which set him up from the beginning of the evening to see the situation from his trance's perspective, to be emotionally dependent on Janet in order to feel safe, worthy of love, and fulfilled. His trance reality made her his source of well-being. Naturally, then, when she directed her interest, joy, and playfulness toward someone else, it felt to him like she was yanking away his emotional lifeline. Jealousy always boils down to some version of this basic trance dynamic.

Ordinarily, Janet has enough personal resources and emotional clarity to not react to William's insecurity by entering a defensive trance, although she does have to pay close attention to her tendency to feel hurt when misjudged. But in her moderately intoxicated state, which is a trance of its own, her discernment and sensitivity were impaired, and she was more easily triggered into a contracted emotionally reactive state. This, combined with the disinhibiting effects of alcohol, simply overwhelmed her capacity to stay in full present awareness, where she would have had the emotional resources and clarity she needed.

> **Avoidant trances do not lead to resolution or learning because they are designed for self-protection, based upon fearful patterns of perception and belief.**

There is no resolution to be had as long as they remain entranced. Avoidant trances do not lead to resolution or learning because they are designed for self-protection, based upon fearful patterns of perception and belief. They do not allow authentic encounters precisely because such encounters can only occur when two people are fully present and willing to be vulnerable. It is obvious in this example that neither Janet nor William were able to acknowledge or reveal the tender truth of their feelings in the moment. Both were too ensnared in the emotional drama (or trance) of defending and justifying themselves.

Let us consider another example.

Linda and Connie are both in their forties. Connie has a daughter from a prior marriage who is away at college. Linda has no children and lived alone for several years before meeting and falling in love with Connie. Having lived together for almost six years, they had gone through their share of ups and downs but, for the most part, enjoyed a happy and loving home life together. For the past few months, though, their relationship seemed strained and they were arguing more than usual.

Both Linda and Connie have demanding, stressful careers, and they really needed a vacation. They heard about a charming inn located in a remote scenic mountain area, which appealed to both of them as a place of natural beauty, quiet relaxation, and a place where they could nurture their relationship. Though they expected that the drive would require some careful map reading and navigating, they calculated that they could make the trip in a day. They scheduled a week off work, and had been talking nonstop about the trip for days before they left.

The plan was to get an early start the first day so they would have a better chance of arriving at the inn before dark. Linda, who generally has a well-planned, methodical approach to the details of her life, had finished packing her clothes and personal items the night before. But Connie had left most of her packing for the morning they were to leave. Linda was anxious to leave early as planned, and was irritated at Connie's last-minute packing frenzy. She was particularly annoyed with Connie because this had happened on numerous other occasions. In fact, already anticipating a frustrating departure, Linda had pleaded with Connie earlier that week to not "pull her usual stunt" of waiting until the last minute to take care of things, causing them to get a late start.

Connie had agreed to pack ahead of time, but somehow the time had slipped away and there she was, packing that morning.

Linda made breakfast for them both but was emotionally distant and cool toward Connie. After all their talking and planning, even emphasizing the need to leave early, Linda was dismayed and wondered how Connie could be so incredibly inconsiderate by not being ready to leave as soon as they got up. Linda had already filled the car up with gas, checked the oil and the tires, and had even packed a lunch and snacks for the trip. She felt as though Connie, by not being ready on time, obviously didn't care about her feelings and needs.

While she was waiting, an old emotional pain seized Linda. In a prior relationship several years ago, Linda had felt invisible to her lover. It hadn't started out that way. There were three or four years of warmth and closeness. But over time, and for reasons Linda never really understood, the relationship cooled off and her partner, Jim, seemed to find everything else in his life more important than Linda. Linda's feelings and needs began to be put aside, at first because of his job, and then because of his need to hang out with his friends or to work on his projects. The relationship became increasingly hostile and Jim ignored Linda or blew her off when she tried to tell him how she felt or what she needed. Ultimately, he left her because of his need for "space from her incessant nagging and control." The fact that Jim filled that space with another woman only a month later didn't help Linda to ever understand or to reconcile what had really happened.

The few years between Linda's relationships had not healed her wound as she had hoped. It had simply gone dormant. The old pain and self-doubt had resurfaced in the strain of the past few months. Connie's apparent disregard for Linda's strong desire to leave early left Linda feeling invisible again, just as she had with Jim. Surely, it was an indication that Connie was on her way out of the relationship, but, just like Jim, couldn't or wouldn't admit it. Now she was faced with the dread of losing love all over again. On the verge of panic, her automatic survival reaction was to flip into a rage trance. And when Connie had the nerve to announce that she was going to do a small load of laundry before they left because she needed a pair of jeans that were dirty, Linda flew over the top. Too angry to speak, her only initial response was an icy stare.

Connie knew she was "in trouble." And she was afraid of Linda's anger. But she also resented having to do everything Linda's way. Maybe she had agreed to pack early, but she couldn't help it if other things had come up that she had to take care of. She thought Linda was often too rigid and controlling. But she had never voiced this to her. It had never felt safe to do so. Why couldn't Linda just get off her back!

This all felt just like the way her mother treated her when she was a child, demanding that Connie be more organized and prompt, and criticizing her when she wasn't. The few times Connie argued with her mother that she was being unfair, she was scolded harshly and then given a cold shoulder for several hours, which was devastating to her. Connie learned that it was safer to simply apologize and promise her mother she would do better. Yet, even though Connie thought her promise was sincere, she never seemed to be able to change her behavior. Her mother interpreted this as defiance and disrespect. Connie was kind of puzzled herself, as she was not consciously trying to defy her mother. But she had to admit (if only to herself) that she felt a secret satisfaction in her mother's inability to fully control her.

Absorbed in their trance, they lost conscious awareness of who they were as souls, causing their love to be temporarily inaccessible.

All it took to activate that old trance state was for Linda to give her that cold hostile stare, and Connie felt all over again the shame and the resentment of her childhood. And what made matters worse, Connie felt no wiser or better equipped to fix this now with Linda than she did when she was a child with her mother. Her frustration simply added to her shame, and her fear of Linda's obvious rage rendered Connie unable to speak directly to Linda about what was going on with her. Connie finished packing quickly—including her dirty jeans—amid the palpable tension in the silence between them. A silence broken only by a couple of one-word sentences and a slammed door. It wasn't until they finally got in the car and were driving that they began to slowly and painfully sort out what was really going on. But that happened only after all hell broke loose, and only after they were able to regain full present awareness.

Even though Linda and Connie truly love each other, they were reduced to adversaries by their shared trance reality, where the emotional stakes were painfully high and there was no possibility of anyone emerging without further wounding. It was the very opposite of what they both wanted and needed—for themselves and for the relationship. Absorbed in their trance, they lost conscious awareness of who they were as souls, causing their love to be temporarily inaccessible.

However, not all complementary dysfunctional trance patterns escalate into an argument. Every couple has their own set of trances and styles of interaction. Some trances feel more like a heavy cloud hanging over the relationship that rarely, if ever, erupts into a storm. Sometimes, one or both become emotionally withdrawn in the course of a trance, or create all sorts of distractions in order to avoid confrontation. Sometimes, a shared trance can quietly spiral down into a feeling of despair, hopelessness, or resignation. Let us now revisit our first couple.

Three and a half years after Jessie and Patrick met, they decided to live together. Neither of them felt drawn to be legally married, each for their own reasons. But they loved each other and felt a deep commitment to their relationship, as well as to their gradually evolving project of creating a sustainable, eco-friendly, intentional community. It was a year after Jessie moved in with Patrick that an especially painful trance emerged between them that neither had recognized before.

The owner of the nursery that Jessie managed decided to sell the nursery, and gave Jessie the first option to buy. In almost every way, this opportunity was a dream come true for Jessie. The only concern had to do with Jessie's financial ability to come up with a sufficient down payment that would allow her to afford the subsequent mortgage payments. She needed considerably more money than she currently had at her disposal, and this was a source of anxiety.

Initially, Jessie was excited to share the news with Patrick. She was also appreciative of his suggestions about how she could approach certain lending companies, given her financial limitations. She was also relieved when she learned from Patrick how she might structure an alternative proposal to the owner which would require much less "up front" money. But when, over the course of a month or two, these suggestions didn't seem to be panning out, Jessie's initial anxiety returned and intensified.

For the next couple of weeks, Jessie talked in great detail with Patrick about her frustrations in her attempts to secure the deal, and her growing fear that she might not be able to make it happen. Patrick listened attentively and continued to offer suggestions about how she might proceed. But, after several of these conversations, something began to feel not right. Patrick acted more distant than usual. And the more agitated Jessie felt, the more aloof Patrick seemed in his responses. At first, Jessie only felt mildly puzzled by Patrick's responses. But this soon festered into hurt and disappointment that he didn't seem interested in supporting her emotionally.

Jessie was not sleeping well, and the muscles in her shoulders were so tightly knotted that they felt like rocks. She felt dismissed when all Patrick would do was to offer her more suggestions and tell her to try not to worry about it so much. In her hurt and dismay, Jessie withdrew emotionally from Patrick and quit talking about the situation or her feelings. This did not help matters. In her silent withdrawal, Jessie became more obsessive about her situation and began to ruminate about Patrick.

Lying in bed after Patrick had fallen asleep, questions would haunt her. "How could he be so insensitive? Does he not see how painfully I am struggling? Does he not see me sinking into a dark hole?" Or alone in the shower, "His suggestions were okay for a while, but obviously aren't panning out. Patrick has far more financial resources than me. Why doesn't he offer to give me or, at least, loan me the money? He has never seemed stingy before. Does he have some hang-up about money that I just haven't seen before?" But with these questions, Jessie also felt a wave of shame. Was she looking for a hand out, for pity? The very thought of that disgusted her.

Jessie was not certain that she was interpreting Patrick's behavior accurately, but because she felt shame about her financial inadequacy and her emotional desperation, she did not voice any of these questions or concerns to Patrick. When Patrick asked her for an update, she responded curtly and said only that it was still in progress. Patrick rarely followed up with a more probing question. It seemed to Jessie that Patrick was relieved not to have to listen to her personal struggle, which only deepened her feelings of shame and isolation.

It all came to a head one evening as Jessie was driving home from work. The real wound at the core of her crisis finally revealed itself to her. She didn't want to go home immediately, so she decided to take a much longer route that meandered through the countryside. Her ruminations had resumed as usual, but soon plunged to a much deeper level. "Does he just not love me enough to offer some direct financial help? Can he not see that I can't do this by myself!" With this question, she began to sob uncontrollably and had to pull her car off the road.

Amidst the sobbing, a voice rose up from some place deep within her, a voice so heartbroken, so innocent, so young, it took her completely by surprise. "I can't do this without you!" she yelled. "I need you!" the young voice pleaded between the heaving. "How could you just leave me here all alone?" It wasn't just the voice that surprised her, or even the depth of her heartbreak. It was that she was no longer thinking about Patrick. The plea wasn't to him at all. It was to her father, her daddy, whom she loved and needed. It was for him that she utterly longed. But she could not have him now, just as she could not have him most of her life.

What is not healed because of denial or avoidance tends to become frozen in its unhealed state.

Jessie wept harder and deeper. She wept the way she couldn't when, at six years old, her mother told her that her daddy had been in a car accident and had died. The emotional shock was too great, the devastation was simply too overwhelming, for that little girl. Now, in the car, Jessie could not hold back, could no longer keep her grief contained. She wept until she was completely spent. A while later, she was able to compose herself enough to drive home.

This example shows how avoidant trances that were formed early in life can re-emerge and leak into our daily life years later. Humans are highly adaptive by nature. When necessary, we will almost always find one way or another to adapt to circumstantial changes or emotional crises. That does not mean that certain types of adaptation do not have challenging or problematic consequences. We can only have compassion for Jessie, as a little girl, not having the personal resources to fully comprehend, much less accept, the loss of her father.

Ideally, both parents can provide their children with the emotional protection and support needed to help them to not be so overwhelmed in times of crisis. Unfortunately, Jessie's crisis was compounded by the fact that it was her father who had been her primary source of emotional support. Her mother always seemed to be struggling with her own problems, and was not usually emotionally available. This left Jessie with nowhere to turn. No one's arms in which she felt safe to fall apart. Her self-protective adaptation to avoid the full emotional impact of her shattering loss happened like reflex, and without ever fully realizing it, she entered a state of partial denial, or an avoidant trance state.

As is generally the case, what is not healed because of denial or avoidance tends to become frozen in its unhealed state. As long as the avoidant trance remains intact, the original wound will remain mostly hidden from our direct conscious awareness, and therefore, cannot be healed. Jessie's experience as a terrified and brokenhearted little girl had never become integrated into the rest of who she was as an emotionally mature adult. Her current circumstances simply reactivated that earlier traumatic experience.

As an avoidant trance begins to dissolve, the emotional crisis is free to emerge into our full present awareness, often with the same tone, texture, and intensity as the original experience. But in our full present adult consciousness, we are far more able to experience such intensity without being so overwhelmed that we are forced to shut down emotionally. Instead, we can accept and integrate the experience into a larger sense of who we are. This is what occurred with Jessie.

In the meantime, though, certain aspects of her trance behavior triggered one of Patrick's trances, which he had simultaneously projected into their relationship. This did not become apparent to him until the same night of Jessie's breakthrough.

Patrick had been feeling the growing tension and the distance between Jessie and himself. He knew Jessie was preoccupied with getting a loan but could not understand why she was so intensely emotional about it. He very much wanted Jessie to be able to purchase the nursery. Not only was he sure she would be great as the new owner, he also imagined that the creative freedom to develop the nursery in her own way would bring her much joy and fulfillment. He thought he had offered useful information. This seemed like a time to be excited, so the intensity of Jessie's anxiety and agitation confused him. And, as it continued, Patrick became annoyed and impatient with her, without fully understanding, or being aware of, the real reason for his increasingly intense reaction to her anxiety.

He was concerned when Jessie didn't come home at her usual time. She hadn't said anything about being late. While waiting for her to come home, he began to experience a familiar, awful, sick feeling in the pit of his stomach. It was the same thing he felt about ten years earlier when his younger sister, Emily, was in serious trouble. Ever since her childhood, there were times when Emily was sad or depressed for days or weeks at a time. Even with professional help, Emily struggled through high school and into college. By her junior year of college, she had become dependent on alcohol and cocaine to manage her dark moods. She began to miss too many classes, and finally dropped out. She would cycle between doing fairly well for a while and then going into hiding and seclusion for days. She always struggled financially. At times, she would reach out to Patrick, calling late at night, sometimes high, sometimes hysterical or in a panic. Patrick tried everything he knew to help her and to encourage and support her, but his help never seemed to be enough.

Then, one winter night, Emily called and left Patrick an anguished voice message. It was very late when he got home and listened to her message. While he could tell Emily clearly was in pain, she also sounded drunk. Patrick was frustrated with Emily and very tired that night. He decided not to call her back until the next day, rationalizing that she had probably passed out by now anyway. That night Emily committed suicide. Patrick never forgave himself.

So, when Jessie didn't come home until late, Patrick thought of Emily. He also remembered how helpless and hopeless he had felt. Patrick realized that as Jessie had been acting more and more agitated over the past few weeks, sounding even desperate at times, his heart just automatically shut down. He loved Jessie, and the last thing he wanted was to shut her out of his heart in her time of need. He was just frozen in the pain of his past heartbreak and self-judgment, which he had never allowed to heal. With this awareness, a deep wave of sadness moved through him. And, with the sadness came a genuine and humble feeling of remorse that began to melt his defenses and soften his heart. It softened him toward Emily. It softened him toward himself. It softened him toward Jessie.

By the time Jessie got home, they were both in a place where they were able to reconnect in a warm and loving way, and to honestly share with each other the deeper pain and unhealed wounds that had recently emerged in their relationship. The drama that seemed so real just a while ago now felt more like a bad dream that they had both just awakened from. Humbled, encouraged, and renewed, their relationship grew to a whole new level.

Once he became fully conscious of the true source of his emotional pain and allowed himself to feel it for what it was, he was released from the automatic grip of his avoidant trance.

As we can see from this story, once Jessie's true crisis of the grief over her father's death was allowed into her present adult awareness, the trance that she had projected into her relationship with Patrick dissolved. The same was true for Patrick. Once he became fully conscious of the true source of his emotional pain and allowed himself to feel it for what it was, he was released from the automatic grip of his avoidant trance. At that point, he could distinguish between his relationship with Emily and his relationship with Jessie, and both now had the freedom that comes from full present awareness to choose to no longer project onto each other.

In each of the stories in this chapter, Janet and William, Linda and Connie, and Jessie and Patrick, the six characteristics of a trance are evident. We can see how easily and seamlessly one or both partners can slip into a trance and stay trapped in it for some time. From the outside looking in, it is apparent how the projections of our trances automatically distort a true knowing of our partner and ourselves. Unfortunately, it is not so apparent from the inside.

There are times when one or the other person spontaneously wakes up from their trance, as in the example of Jessie and Patrick. In those instances, it may be enough simply to experience the relief from the contracted state of consciousness and to recognize the distress of our emotional or interpersonal reactivity for the trance state that it is. When that occurs, a sense of peace, gratitude, and compassion naturally follows. But since one of the characteristics of a trance is that we don't ordinarily know we are in one, we are not usually looking for anything beyond confirmation of our own trance experience. And because a trance tends to remain intact until it runs its full course or is interrupted, it can seem as if we are at the mercy of forces and influences outside our conscious awareness to free us from our contracted experience.

This is how we so often experience our lives. But it is not how it has to be, or needs to be. We can choose to wake up! And this process begins when we make it our conscious intent to live a deeply present and aware life. Once we are grounded in this intent, we are ready to develop a practice of awakening that can be cultivated, practiced, and honed along the way.

CHAPTER FOUR

4

An Individual Practice of Awakening

Once we realize that the primary sources of our interpersonal problems are the individual and shared trances in which we are engaged, the nature of our healing work changes significantly. We realize that the culprit is neither our partner, nor ourselves, but the trance(s) in which either or both of us are ensnared. Rather than attempting to correct or improve ourselves (or more futile, attempting to impose such corrections on our partner), we can focus our attention and efforts on one central question: Am I, in this moment, awake?

This is such a crucial question because as long as we are unwittingly operating from our trance state, any solution or intervention we try will be limited, if effective at all, because it will be a product of the same mindset which created the problem in the first place. We may or may not have the clarity of an immediate answer to this central question, but whenever a challenging moment arises between ourselves and our partner, the simple act of honestly asking ourselves, "Am I, in this moment, awake?" is like pushing a "restart" button on our interpretation of the situation, and our perspective.

Asking this question as a genuine inquiry also makes explicit our *intent* to be awake and anchors it in the present moment, the same moment in which we might well already be in a trance. But before we are likely to feel motivated to engage in a disciplined practice of awakening, we need to acquaint ourselves with the range of our own trance states. Keeping a journal for the sole purpose of recording every trance you enter and are able to identify is a relatively simple and concrete way to begin. It can be quite revealing to take a given period of time: a week, a day, or even just a few hours, and try to identify the variety of trance states you enter. Most people are amazed to discover how much of their time is spent in one trance or another.

Of course, not entering a dysfunctional trance at all is ideal, but such presence of mind does not usually come without a considerable degree of self-awareness and observational skills. Fortunately, for myself and for most people with whom I have worked, the self-awareness and observational skills that we need are not that difficult to cultivate and hone once we enter an intentional *practice of awakening.*

> The self-awareness and observational skills that we need are not that difficult to cultivate and hone once we enter an intentional *practice of awakening.*

Such a practice must begin with the clear intent to be awake. This may seem obvious, but throughout our practice there will be other motivations and impulses that will compete with, or divert us from, our intent to be awake if we are not well anchored in it. Every trance that we seek to awaken from is sustained by its own particular intent, whether it is to feel safe, or justified, or in control, or numb, or righteous, or satisfied in some way. To avoid being distracted, seduced, alarmed, or lulled by the very trances we are choosing to be conscious of will require an equally powerful intent to be awake.

Three Skills Needed for Awakening

Once we are anchored in the clear intent to be awake, there are three essential skills needed for a practice of awakening. First, to be able to identify or *recognize* the trance we are in. Second, to be able to carefully *observe* (as a witness) the subjective experience of the trance as it unfolds. Third, to be able to *shift* the weight of our personal identification from the reactive trance identity to our observing self, the self rooted in full present awareness. These three skills: *recognition, observation,* and *shifting* represent the foundation of a practice of awakening. They first will be presented incrementally in order to facilitate the learning of each skill, but once learned, the tasks will be most effective when practiced as part of a continuous and free-flowing process.

We also need to remember that these skills must be developed by each of us individually, independent of our respective partners. As our mastery of these skills develops, they easily can be integrated into a shared practice of awakening, which will be described in chapter 5. But, whether we are alone or with our partner, our trance states represent our unique private realities, from which we alone need to awaken. Ultimately, the path of awakening is our own, even when we choose to share the journey with a partner. Waking up together means waking up together, as two whole people.

Central to the act of waking up is the ability to recognize when we are in a trance. **Recognition** must be the ***first skill*** needed for our practice because if we do not realize that we are in a trance, we will not know that there is anything to wake up from. This presents us with a conundrum from the very beginning. As stated in chapter 2, one of the characteristics of a trance is that, generally speaking, when we are in one, we don't know it. That is because we are absorbed in its contents, and perceive reality through the distorted lens of our trance.

The problem is that while our experience is filtered through the lens created by whatever trance we happen to be in, the lens itself usually remains invisible to us. So, when we are in a trance, we do not generally think to ourselves, "Hmm. Isn't this an interesting trance I am in, giving me this unique set of feelings, perceptions, and assumptions about myself and reality." Instead, we simply experience what we experience as reality, or the way things are, without questioning its source or its relativity. If, for instance, the trance I am in interprets your behavior as hostile, it will not likely occur to me that there is any interpretation going on. I will simply assume you really are hostile. You may or may not actually be hostile, but as long as my perception is filtered through the lens of my trance, I will not be able to discern the difference between how you really are and what I may be projecting onto you. This makes recognition a slippery and challenging skill to learn.

> Central to the act of waking up is the ability to recognize when we are in a trance.

What we need, then, is to become attuned and sensitive to the cues that would inform us as to whether we are fully present and awake, or in a trance. Those clues will be found by stepping back from the specific content of our thoughts, feelings, and perceptions of a given moment, and refocusing our attention more broadly on the general *nature and quality* of our subjective experience. The nature and quality of our experience when we are fully present and awake will be in sharp contrast to the subjective experience of a trance. Having a clear grasp of the *characteristics of trance states*, as presented in chapter 2, will provide a helpful frame of reference that will provide assistance with recognizing the difference. I recommend re-reading that chapter as often as necessary to feel at home with this information, which may seem a bit overwhelming at first. You can also refer to the appendix on p. 120 for a quick-glance summary.

As a general rule, we could consider any automatic or recurring pattern of consciousness that distorts or diminishes full present awareness of our true self as a likely candidate for being a trance. A dysfunctional avoidant (or reactive) trance will usually reveal itself in the form of certain strong impulses or feelings of need. Whereas, when we are truly awake, our experience is complete unto itself, so that we generally do not experience ourselves as lacking or needing anything essential. For a quick reference in any given moment, the following checklist of the nature and qualities of subjective experience can be used to highlight the contrast between a fully awake state of consciousness and an entranced state of consciousness. Are we awake, or asleep at the wheel?

Characteristics of Being Psychologically and Spiritually Awake

- An underlying sense of peace, free of any emotional reactivity
- Full present-oriented awareness of our internal and external experience
- An open, humble, and receptive quality of heart

Characteristics of Being in an Avoidant or Reactive Trance

There will be a strong impulse or perceived need to do any of the following:

- Guard, defend, or justify ourselves
- Blame, control, or change our partner or ourselves
- Run away, hide, or disappear

Many of the trances we enter are simple, discrete, and naturally contained within a specific circumstance, which tends to make them short-lived. I have found it helpful to describe a trance as being like a room in the "home" of your mind. Every trance, just like a room, has an entrance, an interior space, and an exit. For some, it is easiest to begin learning how to recognize our trances in retrospect using this analogy.

The *entrance* represents the circumstance, event, sensory experience, memory, or interaction that triggered the trance. The *interior space* contains a primary emotional tone or feeling, such as fear, anger, sadness, guilt, dread, etc. It usually will by supported by an underlying theme containing a belief, assumption, or interpretation about life, or our predicament or position, such as "He/she/they don't like me"; "I'm stupid/incompetent"; "You can't trust people"; "They want something from me"; "I can't win for losing"; "Life is unfair or unsafe"; "I don't have enough time"; or, "What if . . . (filled in with some type of catastrophe)."

Many of my clients have found it quite helpful to name each trance according to its primary feeling tone or theme, such as my *resentment* trance; my *victim* or *martyr* trance; my *hurt little boy* trance; my *road rage* trance; my *addictive* trance; or, my *distrusting* trance. Naming our trances in this way not only makes it easier to identify them as they arise, but also tends to objectify them, thereby giving us a little breathing room or space between the trance identity and who we are as the observer.

> **Every trance, just like a room, has an entrance, an interior space, and an exit.**

We may, at first, find it nearly impossible to realize we are in a trance while we are in the midst of it. But once we are no longer in our trance, we may be better able to think back and find the point or circumstance that triggered our entry into the trance. Likewise, after we have awakened from our trance, the contrast in the quality of our experience should be noticeable and will likely make it easier to identify the moment or situation that served as our exit. Identifying the entrances and exits to our dysfunctional trance states allows us to become more skillful at anticipating them, and in some cases, learning not to enter them, at all.

Once we have enough familiarity with trances to begin to recognize when we are engaged in one, the first question that often arises is, "Now what?" This question arises out of the fact that simply being aware of our trance does not necessarily wake us up—at least not entirely. One can be very aware that he or she is trapped in an angry or insecure trance identity, for instance, but still feel dominated by the anger or insecurity. Recognition is fundamental and necessary, but not always sufficient. So just how do we go about the task of waking up? What tools, skills, or approach is needed to move beyond mere recognition of our various trance states to actually waking up?

This brings us to the ***second skill*** in our practice of awakening, which is to carefully **observe** the trance experience as it unfolds, including the emotional reactions and behavioral patterns that are generated within the trance state. We might think of this process as getting to know the interior experience of our trance consciously and intimately. It is important to note that, in our observation, we are not attempting to assess, change, theorize, or generalize about our trance. It is more like watching a movie or "peeking in" on our dream. For many of us, this involves accessing a new kind of observational skill, a kind of meta-awareness that allows us to notice and feel our trance reactions without becoming completely fused with them. The quality of this observation might best be described as dispassionate, nonattached, and neutral watching. It is as if we need a second set of eyes, not belonging to the trance identity, which allows us to focus on the *process* of the trance without identifying with, or being invested in, its *contents*. Essentially, what we need is to cultivate our ability to access two states of consciousness at the same time.

. . . to carefully **observe** the trance experience as it unfolds, including the emotional reactions and behavioral patterns that are generated within the trance state.

This may seem like an obscure and daunting skill to develop because we usually don't think this way. But fortunately, it is an innate ability that simply needs to be practiced for it to begin to feel natural. Meditation is perhaps the most common practice that intentionally cultivates this quality of observational skill. Vipassana meditation and other forms of *mindfulness* practice are particularly suited for this. There are many excellent books, audio recordings, and workshops on vipassana and mindfulness practice offered by prominent teachers, such as Thich Nhat Hanh, Pema Chodron, Jack Kornfield, Jon Kabat-Zinn, Joseph Goldstein, Joan Borysenko, and others. If you are experienced and comfortable with any form of meditation or mindfulness practice that cultivates "the witness," or "observer," you may find that your practice is similar and easily adaptable to the practice of recognizing, observing, and ultimately waking up from a trance state.

For those not familiar with the phenomenon of the observer or witness and find the concept hard to get a handle on, there is an experiential way to get a feel for this aspect of consciousness. For a short period of time, perhaps fifteen minutes, imagine that you are asleep and dreaming your experience. There is no need to do anything different than what you would ordinarily do during that time. Your only task is to imagine that you are inside a dream that just happens to exactly match what would ordinarily be occurring during those fifteen minutes. Notice and watch every aspect of this "dream" as it unfolds: your thoughts and feelings and physical sensations, how you interact with others, how your body moves, etc. You must be conscious and intentional about imagining this or you will forget you are doing it almost as soon as you begin.

If you would like to practice this exercise, you could take a moment now, for instance, as you are reading the following paragraphs. It is helpful to do this exercise with a light, playful, inquisitive attitude. Remember, you are creating a "what if" scenario in order to exercise part of your mind. If you take it too seriously, you will more than likely get bogged down.

Begin by imagining that you are sound asleep in your bed right now and that the experience you are having this moment—of reading this book—is actually just a dream. You've just now "shown up" inside this dream, so to speak. It is a dream that could easily have gone unnoticed or unrecognized as a dream since it appears exactly the same as any ordinary moment in your waking life. But for this exercise, you are imagining that you do realize that you are dreaming.

Now, take a moment to orient yourself in this "dream." You might first take note of your immediate environment. Where are you dreaming that you are as you read this? At home in your den, bedroom, bathroom? Or, are you dreaming that you are at a café during your lunch break? Is it daytime or evening? What is the weather like? Is it warm or cold? All of this can be thought of as the setting inside your dream or your "dreamscape."

To further anchor yourself in this "dream," bring your attention to your body. Are you sitting in a chair or on a couch or sitting up in bed? Notice any tension, pressure, itching, or soreness.

Notice any pleasant sensations, as well, such as warmth or coolness or relaxation. Are you sipping on a drink as you read this? If so, take a swallow and really pay attention to the sensations of taste, temperature and texture as the liquid enters your mouth and moves down your throat. Wiggle your toes, stretch, take a deep breath and let yourself sigh as you exhale. Notice the weight and texture of this book that you are holding, and the position of your hand and fingers. Feel the variety of these sensations and keep reminding yourself that these are the physical sensations you are experiencing in your dream.

Now that you have identified the setting and your physical experience of this dream, go one step further and identify any particular story or drama that you may be engaged in, or problem or issue you are currently facing. It can be at work, at home, or in a particular relationship. Don't attempt to analyze or change anything. Simply take a brief inventory of any strong opinions or positions you may identify with, and any emotional reactions that this issue or drama evokes in you.

All of these directions are simply to bring your attention to this moment in your life from a fresh and original perspective. Everything you are noticing and identifying represent the textures, qualities, and perceptions, as well as the narrative aspects of your dream. Notice how real it all looks and feels. Take a moment to let this experience settle in. Muse a bit and linger in the felt sense of this "dream" experience to become even more familiar with it.

When you are ready, let yourself "wake up" from this imaginary dream. You may feel a little disoriented so it is a good idea to "de-role" when you are ready to end any deeply imagined exercise like this. That is, remind yourself that this was just an exercise and you are now finished and no longer in the "dream." Make sure that you feel grounded before you go on to something else. That's all you need to do for now.

For some, this exercise stimulates a dramatic shift of perspective. For others, the shift is subtle. If you do not immediately get the hang of it, there is no need for concern. Just play with it from time to time. You might be pleasantly surprised.

By *imagining* what is actually occurring, we will be creating an experiential paradox (How could an experience be both real and imagined at the same time?). That paradox disrupts the automatic nature of our experience. The disruption loosens the grip of our ordinary state of consciousness, which is mono-dimensional and assumes reality to be one thing, and creates the space for another state of consciousness to emerge simultaneously. This exercise can be of enormous benefit in accessing and cultivating the witness or observer aspect of our awareness. The more often we practice it, in a variety of situations and for different lengths of time, the more fluid and nimble our consciousness will become. This is a powerful exercise and can be a little disorienting at first. Therefore, it is not recommended while driving or using dangerous machinery. Otherwise, if it doesn't create too much anxiety or mental confusion, we likely will find it fascinating, even entertaining.

Once we get a feel for being in two states of consciousness simultaneously, it will seem more natural to both recognize and observe our trance states. By training our attention toward the close and intimate observation of that specialized experience, something remarkable begins to happen. The aspect of our awareness that does the observing begins to feel familiar, more consistently available, and implicitly trustworthy. In time, this observing consciousness may deepen and expand and may ultimately be experienced as no longer simply a mental function, but an intrinsic aspect of who we are.

This sets the stage for the ***third skill*** in our practice of awakening, which is to **shift** our primary identification from the trance to the aspect of ourselves that is observing the trance. The shift may be subtle at first because it is simply a matter of emphasis. It is much like standing on both legs, one being your identification with the contents and identity of the trance, and the other being the observer of that trance. Most of your weight may be on the trance leg, with just a little weight on the observer leg. By placing more of your attention on the experience of observing, you will be shifting the weight and focus of your personal identification to that leg. Whereas, perhaps only moments before, you were mainly in the trance with just a little conscious awareness of it, you now are acutely aware of the trance, but feeling much less defined and possessed by it.

To the degree you are fused with the trance, you only have access to the resources, the perceptual range, and the intent of that trance. But the observer aspect has no agenda other than awareness, which is based in the present. So, to the degree you are consciously observing your trance, you have access to all of the resources that are available in full present awareness. These resources either can serve to create more clarity and choice within the trance, or may even serve to dissipate the trance altogether.

Stalking Our Trances

Some trance patterns are so subtle, illusive, or camouflaged as ordinary experience that we do not see them for what they are until we are already ensnared in them, much like a bug in a spider's web. Other trances are more immediately disruptive and overpower us like a wild animal pouncing upon its prey. In either case, we are caught off guard and are at a real disadvantage in our attempts to get—and remain—free of our trances. For this reason, it is important not to wait until we are already in a trance to engage our practice of awakening. Rather, we need to be proactive when we are awake so that we are not simply at the mercy of our trances when they strike.

These resources either can serve to create more clarity and choice within the trance, or may even serve to dissipate the trance altogether.

One way to facilitate this, after we have gone through the initial process of identifying and naming our trances, is to develop the art of *stalking our trances*. To do this, we need to start with a focused intent to find and identify a given trance while we are still awake. The archetype of the *stalker* invokes an attitude of intense curiosity and genuine intrigue about the workings of our own trances. As the stalker, we do not simply wait for a trance to emerge but actively seek it out. We will be on the lookout for signs and clues that would indicate that a trance is beginning (or potentially beginning) to emerge. We will be sensitizing and honing our attention as if learning to catch the "scent" of a particular emotional reaction or impulse, noticing any change in our own thoughts and behaviors. For example, our tone of voice or the use of a particular figure of speech, or the emergence of a strong opinion or emotionally charged assumption, or the onset of any number of physical sensations.

All trances occur within a context of some kind, whether internal or external, and are, therefore, associated with specific circumstances, behaviors, environments, memories, or types of relationships, such as family of origin, social, or work communities, etc. From the stalker's perspective, the context and any of the associated elements of a trance represents its "habitat" or natural environment. In order to stalk a trance, we must begin our search in the environment where it is most likely to occur. For instance, in order to stalk our "road rage" trance, we would begin our search while we are driving (or anytime we might be thinking about driving and begin to feel that rage). If we were stalking our "anxiety at work" trance, we would begin our search while at work. If we were stalking a trance related to our family of origin, we would begin stalking while at a family gathering or, perhaps, when we were having a conversation on the telephone with a parent or sibling—as these are the circumstances in which those trances are activated.

> **As the stalker, we do not simply wait for a trance to emerge but actively seek it out.**

About twenty years ago I had an experience that exemplifies this process, although I had not yet formalized the concept or practice of stalking trances. Up until that time, I had been troubled by a particular trance associated with receiving shots. As a child I never liked getting a shot but at some point, my aversion intensified into an anxiety trance so overpowering that I would faint almost every time I received a shot or had my blood drawn. This continued for several years throughout college and into my early adulthood. As annoying and inconvenient as it was, my "fainting" trance was so predictable that I could warn doctors and nurses before they would administer a shot, and they would gratefully have me lie down first. The anxiety was not about the pain, which was usually minimal and short lived. It came from something deeper emotionally and less obvious to me. While I could speculate as to its origin, I found that it wasn't necessary because by this time the trance seemed to get triggered automatically with no conscious association or memory of its origin.

My growing frustration about fainting prompted me to want to understand it better so that hopefully I could be done with it. During one appointment when I was scheduled to have my blood drawn, I shared my dilemma of fainting with my doctor and told him I really wanted to get to the bottom of the problem. I told him I had an idea of what I needed, which was to be left alone in a room after my blood was drawn so that I could explore what was really happening in me that was causing me to faint. Fortunately, my doctor was a personal friend as well as a generous and open-minded physician. He was glad to accommodate me, and instructed his staff to leave me alone in my room after my blood had been drawn.

Normally, I would have dreaded having my blood drawn, knowing how unpleasant the aftermath always was. But this time I was so committed to getting to the bottom of this problem, I was actually looking forward to the experience of fainting. As soon as my blood was drawn, my doc wished me luck and left me alone. In acute anticipation, I waited, watching for the first hints of fainting. Sure enough, I began to feel that familiar clammy, sweaty feeling—but this was good, I thought. I was on it! Then came that familiar metallic taste in my mouth that accompanied the onset of nausea. Now, I was really excited—I was going to catch the faint at the exact point it occurred. I waited and watched and tuned in acutely so I could track even the subtlest intensification of any of the sensations, as this was how I would "close in" on the faint. I continued to wait—watching, scanning for the sensations. But they didn't intensify. In fact, the more I sought them out, the less intense they became. I began to get mildly impatient. For the first time, I was truly ready and intent on facing down my demon. Yet, it seemed that the more I genuinely wanted to meet it, the more illusive it became. Within just a few minutes, there was no trace of anxiety and absolutely no inclination to faint.

This was a rather odd and perplexing experience. Part of me was relieved because I seemed to have broken the spell of fainting. But part of me was genuinely disappointed because I really wanted to find the source of the anxiety that made me faint. Then it occurred to me that the source of the anxiety was my aversion and avoidance of the experience of fainting. Paradoxically, my genuine intent to confront and fully experience the source of the anxiety was the very thing that neutralized it.

The irony of stalking our own trances is that rather than attempting to avoid or end a particular trance, we are actually hoping to come upon it just as it is becoming active, but to do so while we are in our full present awake state. By anchoring ourselves in the stalker archetype, we will be giving ourselves the advantage of being centered and grounded in an awake state as we encounter our trances. This will not guarantee that we never get caught in our trances, but it will greatly enhance our ability to recognize and observe them as they occur.

In this particular situation, because of the unique nature of anxiety, stalking my trance had the secondary effect of dispelling it altogether. While such a relief may spontaneously occur in some situations, this is not always the case and is not the point I want to emphasize. Stalking our trances cultivates a degree of mastery in our ability to recognize our trances, whether or not they are neutralized at the time.

Lucid Dreaming

One approach that helps to integrate all three skills into an elegant practice of awakening is based on a phenomenon known as lucid dreaming. Strictly speaking, lucid dreaming refers to a shift of consciousness that occurs when we are asleep and dreaming. While we are in the midst of the dream, we become *aware* that we are dreaming. It is not that we wake up out of our dream, which would mean that the dream stops. Rather, we are waking up inside the dream as it continues. In our ordinary dreams, we are in a scene or story of some kind, and are so absorbed in it that it does not occur to us that we are dreaming. In a lucid dream, we become aware, not only that we are dreaming, but also that the character we are dreaming ourselves to be is not who we actually are, but part of the contents of the dream. This awareness will often prompt a deeper, closely related realization, which is that who we truly are is the one dreaming and, in this moment, the one observing the dream.

When we dream lucidly, we may choose simply to watch what occurs, as this might give us valuable insight into the symbols and meanings of our unconscious mind. But should we wish to engage some aspect of the dream, we can. Knowing that it is our own dream, we can alter or affect the scene or the characters in virtually any way we want. Since the dream is a creative medium of consciousness only, we are neither bound by the laws of gross physical reality, nor of time and space, which ordinarily determine how we manifest change. In our dream we can fly, breath under water, leave our body, talk to animals or spirits, or move through and between scenes simply by remembering that we are dreaming and being clear about what we want. And, this can happen instantaneously the moment a new image or intent occurs to us. Our only real limitations are our awareness and our imagination.

Lucid dreaming can, and often does, occur spontaneously without any preparation or formal knowledge. The experience is usually quite vivid—visually and emotionally—and can have a profound psychological or spiritual impact on the one having it. Accounts of stunning beauty, feelings of ecstatic vibrancy, overwhelming joy, life-changing insights, realizations, and epiphanies are not uncommon when people report their experience of lucid dreaming. Sometimes a difficult life problem is understood in a whole new light from a perspective that had never occurred in that person's ordinary waking consciousness. For some, the experience has the quality of a spiritual gift or revelation, or an answer to prayer. Additionally, a lucid dream can inspire or challenge us to grow philosophically or spiritually, or to learn something or to change something in our waking life. When spontaneous lucid dreams occur, we are likely to be intrigued, and often grateful, simply because the experience is extraordinary and helpful.

I recall one particular lucid dream I had a number of years ago when I was in the throws of a deep spiritual crisis. It was such an extraordinary and compelling dream and had such a surreal poetic quality, I wrote about it afterward. I have included my original writing here to illustrate how we can become aware of our dreaming and our waking life, even while we are still asleep.

> *I stood at the edge of the pond upstream from my campsite beneath a cloudless sky that stretched open and wide and deep into an endless blue. The air blew warm and cool and alive and drew down the sky until it enveloped me in its enormity and I breathed it in and it breathed me in and blew all around the ground and across the surface of the pond. The pond was also blue, bluer than real like a Japanese cartoon and also clear and was so charged with energy that it shot sparks where the sky touched its surface, which was everywhere. The rays of the sun fanned down and out in all directions and illumined everything*

so there were no shadows and everything shimmered; the surface of the pond shimmered thousands of tiny waves and the air shimmered, hushed and nearly invisible and I shimmered inside and out so that nothing was entirely solid, not me, nor the ground, nor the pond.

A man was standing in the middle of the pond; not in the water but on the surface. He was radiant and the air and water around him glistened and he was looking my way. Something quickened within me, at once physical and emotional and vaguely familiar and was urging me toward some wondrous and unreasonable secret, joyful and expectant and willing.

It then dawned on me that this man intended to teach me how to walk on the water. This ought to have been preposterous, but I did not question it. In my eagerness to learn I stepped out onto the surface of the pond. The shimmering of my body had by now become so intense that I felt as though I were a billion particles of light vibrating at an indescribably high speed. The water had an elastic quality and its surface gave slightly as I stepped onto it, but it held me up. Amazed and delighted, I walked out farther. Everything was wildly, ecstatically alive. The entire scene, this world I had somehow entered, was unspeakably and heartbreakingly beautiful.

This man was teaching me without words or explanations. Instead, it seemed as though his vibration was entering my body, attuning me kinesthetically from the inside. It seemed that all I had to do to walk on water was to increase the vibrational rate of the atoms that made up my body to a frequency higher than that of the atoms of which the water was composed. Given this, the molecular bonding at the surface of the water was sufficient to create a natural buoyancy that held up my body.

Of course. How obvious. There was nothing magical or supernatural about it. The "miracle" of walking on water was not in the ability to defy nature but in the awareness of the principles of nature that lay beneath ordinary perception. Nothing was being defied but my conventional perspective of reality. This new awareness was startling and yet, in the moment, completely self-evident. How could I have ever not known this?

I experimented for a while, placing my hands on the surface of the pond, then sitting down and then standing up again. I jumped up and down and rolled over a couple of times, still astounded that the water was holding me up no matter what I did. After a few moments it occurred to me that I was asleep and dreaming. Yet there was still a compelling sense of reality to it. I had a strong feeling that this was a lesson I was supposed to learn. In fact, I thought to myself at one point, "I must take this understanding back with me and remember it when I wake up." With this last thought, the dream ended.

Intentional *lucid dreaming* is also an esoteric spiritual practice that has long been recognized by yogis, mystics, and shamans of various lineages and cultures. There are numerous purposes of lucid dreaming within different traditions, ranging from healing oneself or another to soul travel. But ultimately, the larger purpose of lucid dreaming is to learn about the dream nature of ordinary reality. This is based on one of the common understandings of virtually every esoteric spiritual tradition, which is that, beneath surface appearances, there is far more similarity between our dreamed consciousness and ordinary consensus reality than most of us were taught to believe. Such a view would hold that *reality* as we commonly know it, is far more constructed and relative to a state of consciousness than it is absolute, much like our sleeping dreams. Therefore, if we learn to intentionally lucid dream, that same capacity of lucidity could be applied to our ordinary waking reality, thereby allowing us to live a more spiritually awake life than an unquestioned acceptance of conventional/consensus reality would ever foster.

> *Reality* as we commonly know it, is far more constructed and relative to a state of consciousness than it is absolute.

I have been fascinated with the phenomena of lucid dreaming for many years. It is a broad topic of interest, referenced in literary, spiritual, and scientific works because it stirs the imagination and seems to transcend conventional thinking. How can one be asleep and awake at the same time? It has inspired one of the great mysteries of all time, "What is *reality* vs. a *dream*?" Or, put differently, "Could it be that we are *dreaming* what we experience as *reality*?" Another related question stimulated by the phenomenon of lucid dreaming is, "If we can awaken inside our dream, is there an equivalent experience which relates to our ordinary reality? That is, is our ordinary reality a *dream,* in comparison to some other state, more *awake*?" Esoteric spiritual traditions that emphasize the process of personal initiation, generally provide guidance and assistance by which an initiate addresses these questions at the level of subjective experience.

Traditionally, an adept or apprentice might be given specific instructions for learning how to develop the ability to lucid dream. Don Juan, the legendary Toltec sorcerer, instructed Carlos Castaneda to make his last thought before he fell asleep that he would find his own hands in his dream, and to do this every night for a month. When Carlos finally did notice his hands, this would cue him to remember that he was dreaming. It might take an aspirant or apprentice many persistent attempts to remember before any success is realized. But the potential rewards are many, not the least of which is to see through the illusions of our ordinary waking reality, which we have accepted as truth and which have kept us imprisoned in a very limited state of consciousness.

In his book *The Four Agreements*, Don Miguel Ruiz, continuing in the Toltec perspective, writes about the domestication of human consciousness into consensus reality, referring to it as "*the dream of the planet*." Malcolm Godwin states in his book *The Lucid Dreamer*, "It now appears that Western scientists, in the fundamental disciplines of quantum physics and neurophysiology, are beginning to suspect what the mystics have been saying for thousands of years—that our waking world is like a hologram. It is an illusion. But the ancient traditions also claim that we are capable of creating our dream scenarios, not only in lucid states but in our waking realities as well."

Because a dream is simply a trance we are engaged in while sleeping, those two terms can sometimes be used interchangeably. We could just as easily refer to a trance as a dream we are having while we are physically awake. To avoid unnecessary confusion, I generally use the term *dream* to refer to us as we sleep. However, I have also found it helpful to use the term *waking dream* to refer to a long-standing, pervasive trance state with which we have come to identity over time. Use of language in this way seems to make the principles of lucid dreaming more obviously applicable in our daily life.

Our previous exercise of imagining for a period of time that we are dreaming our experience is a kind of reverse adaptation to the practice of lucid dreaming. It is designed to give us a way to activate and develop one of the abilities of the mind that is so often under-used. Rather than learning how to be awake while we are dreaming, we are learning how to *dream* our *awake* state. The net effect is the same, which is to intentionally access two states of consciousness at the same time. This capacity is a key component in both individual and shared practices of awakening.

In lucid dreaming, we may find ourselves in a position similar to that of an actor/director shooting a scene for a movie. To be effective as an actor, we must enter the role of the character we are portraying so deeply, it is as if we *become* that character. Yet, as the director, we must operate from an altogether different mindset, which involves attending to how the scene is coming together as a whole, and making whatever changes are needed. In a lucid dream, we may wake up inside the character we are dreaming ourselves to be, but we will have the director's mindset. At this point, *recognition, observation*, and *shifting* occur together as a fluid and ongoing process.

The principles of lucid dreaming are compelling whether approached scientifically, spiritually, or metaphorically. The model of lucid dreaming has both immediate and far-reaching implications for couples because it provides a direct and pragmatic way of addressing both the psychological and spiritual aspects of a practice of awakening. In the following two chapters, we will focus primarily on the psychological aspects of relationship and how we can use a model of lucid dreaming as a tool and an invaluable resource for waking up together.

Key Points of an Individual Practice

1. **Recognition:**
   a. Initially, keep a journal or notebook to identify as many trances as possible within a given period of time (a day, a weekend, a week).
   b. Look for and note:
      - the entrance (or triggering event)
      - the primary emotion or feeling tone and theme
      - the exit (or circumstance that facilitated a return to full present awareness)

2. **Observation:**
   a. Bring our attention to the witness aspect of our awareness.
      - The witness is non-judging, non-attached, and has no need to change or resist our experience within the trance.
   b. From the witness state, carefully observe the trance as it unfolds, just as if lucid dreaming.
      - Watch the patterns of thought, feelings, assumptions, judgments, and reactions of the trance state identity.

3. **Shifting:**
      - Shifting is a natural occurrence that begins when we are aware of both our trance and the witness simultaneously.
   a. Do not try to resist, overcome, or get rid of the trance (this would only further imbed us in it, like struggling in quicksand).
   b. Remember that a trance functions as a distorted lens of perception that selects, edits, interprets, and categorizes all information and sensory data according to its own patterns. Therefore, do not give the trance experience credibility for accurately representing an *objective* reality.
   c. Bring more and more attention to the activity of observing, gradually shifting the "weight" of personal identification from the trance identity to the observing Self.
   d. Offer loving forgiveness to the trapped aspect of ourselves as long as it continues to be ensnared in its trances, or waking dreams.

CHAPTER FIVE

A Shared Practice of Awakening

Whether we are alone or with a partner, our practice of awakening is ultimately an individual practice because it is our own trances from which we seek to awaken. But that does not mean it has to occur in isolation. Sharing a practice of awakening can be one of the most rewarding, enriching, and challenging aspects of a couple relationship. A shared practice of awakening gives us a concrete practical framework, as well as a common language for understanding our own and our partner's individual journey. This makes it easier for us to both offer and receive support and encouragement.

A shared practice of awakening also creates a way for our relationship to become both more intimate and more expansive at the same time. On the surface, to describe a relationship using these terms may seem like a contradiction. We usually think of "intimate" as being contained in a private and exclusive interpersonal space, whereas we tend to think of "expansive" as being less contained, more outwardly directed, and more inclusive. And yet, a shared practice of awakening enlarges the context of relationship beyond the narrow limitation of trances often associated with a particular topic or issue, and that lock us into a relatively shallow and narrowed experience of who we are and what our relationship could be. One of the great benefits of a shared practice is that it allows us to experience the depth and freedom of a relationship that is truly present and awake.

There are essentially two levels of a shared practice of awakening. The first level is what I refer to as a *parallel practice*. It is simple, straightforward, and can occur between any two or more people who wish to have a vehicle or forum for both sharing and examining their own individual practice of awakening. A parallel practice can occur between friends, in a small therapy group, or as part of a meditation or spiritual group.* While a parallel practice is not limited to the couple relationship, it is foundational for any shared practice, and is a prerequisite for developing the second level of a shared practice.

The second level of shared practice of awakening is what I refer to as an *interactive practice*. This practice is specific to couples because it focuses on the intimate interactions that are part of the relationship itself in order to move both to a deeper and more complex level of a shared practice. The two levels can and often will occur simultaneously once the foundation of the parallel practice is clearly established. Both practices are built on our individual practice, which simply expands into our relationship.

Level One:
A Parallel Practice

A *parallel practice* assumes that each person is actively engaged in his or her own individual practice of awakening. It is designed explicitly to create a mutually safe interpersonal space so that both partners can be vulnerable and unguarded as they reveal to each other their challenges, insights, missteps, and their discoveries about their individual practice of awakening. We want to develop an atmosphere of camaraderie and mutual support as we each do our own work.

While first developing a parallel practice, it is important that we clearly distinguish this process from an ordinary or casual conversation. There are a number of ways we can do this. Most couples find it helpful to establish a ritual or setting that encourages, supports, and sets apart the practice. For instance, we can designate a particular room in our home or other physical space to be used specifically for sharing our practice.

*Because psychologically or spiritually oriented group dynamics can become intense and emotionally complex rather quickly, it is generally advisable to have a skilled, knowledgeable group leader to facilitate this process.

This should be a neutral space that is pleasant and comfortable for both. We can choose a particular day of the week and/or special time of day. Usually 30–45 minutes, up to an hour is sufficient, once or twice a week, depending on our particular circumstances and needs. We can combine our conversation with an activity that might be conducive to the process, such as going for a walk or a drive. Keep in mind that this is quality time we are dedicating to support, nurture, and/or heal our relationship, so it is important to choose a time when we will be fresh and alert, not when we will be depleted, distracted, or exhausted.

Once a time and place has been established, the practice is simple and straightforward. Each person is to review the week for any of their own trances that were activated, and then take turns sharing with each other how their individual practice of awakening has gone. The following guideline should be helpful.

> The primary gift of a parallel practice is the creation of a sacred interpersonal space in which we can trust intimate exposure to each other without having to defend, justify, or alter our experience.

First, identify each trance by name. If you haven't already named the trance (e.g. related to its circumstance, primary emotional quality, or predominant theme), now is the time to do so. If you need to review this process, it is explained on page 49. *Second*, share with your partner the circumstance or triggering event and what you went through mentally and emotionally, and—if relevant—interpersonally and/or physically. *Third*, share how your individual practice of awakening went. Specifically, think back and try to identify the first moment you realized you were in the trance, and how long and by what means it took to wake up. Or perhaps you might have to report that you have not yet entirely awakened from that particular trance. If so, there is no need to be discouraged or self-critical. After all, realizing that you are still in a trance is part of the practice of awakening.

As we do this, it is important that we share our own process with an open and honest heart, and that we listen to our partner in a non-judgmental and non-competitive spirit. Remember, the parallel practice is designed only to be a sharing of each person's individual practice with the other. It is not intended to be a discussion about analyzing or changing the contents of our trances. Sincere questions asked to elicit further clarification and understanding can be helpful, as can empathetic responses.

But we must refrain from any attempt to change the experience, or advise our partner, or turn the sharing into a problem-solving session. While we might think we are being helpful, it is more likely that such responses would compromise the primary gift of a parallel practice, which is the creation of a sacred interpersonal space in which we can trust intimate exposure to each other without having to defend, justify, or alter our experience.

In a parallel practice, the way in which we listen and respond to our partner's experiences is just as important a part of the practice as the discovery and the sharing of our own experiences. If, as the listener of our partner's experience, we feel the need to correct or enlighten them, we are focusing on their part of the parallel practice instead of doing our part, which is to listen, understand, and to embrace our partner's efforts. Our job is to not intervene. It is important to remember that any need to intervene will likely be an indication that we have become engaged in a trance of our own.

> Because so many of our more dysfunctional trances are triggered in relationships, it is critical that we speak *only of our own trances,* **not** our partner's.

If we discover our own active trance, such as a need for our partner to change or improve in some way, we can do one of two things. We can admit that we are in this moment stuck in a trance, and need to briefly break in order to return to our center. Or, if we are able to shift our balance to the observer, we could share our own trance as part of the parallel practice, remembering that we need to speak out of honest humility rather than from a position of superiority or quiet righteousness.

When first establishing a parallel practice, it is also a good idea to only share the trance states we are discovering that are not directly related to our partner. Because we are new to this process, it is much more challenging to remain open and accepting when what we are hearing involves ourselves. Speaking and listening to matters that are more neutral to the relationship simply makes it less complicated when we are first learning to create a safe sharing space. That being said, this should not limit us too much since most of us are triggered into trance states in many different arenas, and we most likely will have plenty from which to choose that do not directly involve our partner.

When we feel ready to share trances related to our relationship, a cautionary ground rule needs to be established. Because so many of our more dysfunctional trances are triggered in relationships, it is critical that we speak *only of our own trances*, **not** our partner's. This may require a considerable degree of self- discipline because we may be personally invested in the other person waking up from a trance that is causing us trouble! Even if we feel completely justified in our reaction (and usually we will), it will most likely be opinionated and self-serving. In other words, we will be speaking out of a trance of our own.

If we are specifically asked for a response or comment, and we are confident that we are fully present, with an open heart toward our partner, then, an observation may be appropriate and useful. But even then, our comments should be limited to our observations only. Should we start offering our opinion about our partner's behavior, it is very likely that our own self-centered agenda has crept in. And we are asking for an argument, which defeats the whole purpose of sharing our parallel practice.

To help flesh out this practice, consider the following example.

Ellen and David have been living together for three years without any major crises, yet had settled into a lifestyle and routine that felt flat and uninspired. After attending a weekend retreat designed to get a fresh perspective on their relationship, they decided to engage in a shared practice of awakening. David had recently received a tax refund and had not yet decided how he was going to spend it. In celebration of their renewed commitment to enliven their relationship, they agreed to use his refund to purchase a hot tub and set aside a block of time on Sunday mornings in the tub as their ritual space to begin their parallel practice.

They were about four months into their practice when David began one Sunday morning by sharing a particular trance he had been struggling with. "Well, I lost it at work this week."

"What do you mean?"

"I have this one client that is driving me crazy. She has wanted me to photograph an entire line of fabrics plus three collections of pottery to go into her catalog. Several weeks

ago, I recommended a particular way that I thought the photographs would present best in the catalog, including color of background, types of lenses I would use, and the angles that would be most appealing. I spent a lot of time and energy on this! Well, I thought she agreed with my suggestions. But at every step of the way, she has challenged me and second-guessed my judgment. While I know it's her right to, still, it was very annoying. Anyway, two weeks ago she opted to have me do it differently, even though I warned her that I didn't think it was going to create the best look. Then, when I showed her the results this Wednesday, she flipped. She didn't like it at all and started challenging me and berating me."

"My God, David, what did you do?"

"Well, I wanted to cuss her out and tell her to take the photos and shove them! But I managed to control myself and instead told her that we can redo them the way I had originally suggested. That seemed to calm her down a bit.

"But I have been furious ever since. Finally, yesterday, it dawned on me that I was deep in my trance about not being listened to and taken seriously, and feeling very resentful about it. But this also put me in another trance at the same time, one of pure frustration, because now I am behind on another project, as well. These two trances seem to take turns, like tag-team trances, and it makes it real hard to get clear. Even now, I am not completely out of either trance, but they are loosening their grip a little. Actually, talking about it now is helping some."

"That sounds terrible, David. I'm so sorry. And two trances to boot. No wonder you haven't been able to stay fully present yet. I'm amazed you've done as well as you have."

"Thanks. So what about you?"

"I didn't do so great this week."

"Oh?"

"Talking about it feels like a confession."

"Well confess away, my dear. You couldn't have done worse than me."

"I really think you did well, David, all things considered. Anyway, you know how I have been discouraged about not losing weight. I know I don't exercise enough and sometimes I eat too much fattening stuff. But obviously, just knowing that doesn't seem to be enough to get me to change, so I struggle. Yesterday I went to the gym to workout and did okay on the weight machines. But when I started running, I got so exhausted after a mile and a half that I had to stop. I can't tell you how discouraged I felt. I used to be able to run five miles."

"I know that feeling sucks."

"Yeah, but I'm not finished. Then I went into the locker room to shower and looked at myself in the mirror. I hated the way I looked so fat, especially my thighs and my ass. I was so disgusted with myself."

"I love your thighs and your ass."

"I know David, you've told me that before. But I'm trying to tell you about my trance. So don't try to make me feel better right now. Okay?"

"Oops. I'm sorry. I just hate . . ."

"I know. But remember, this is important for me to get through without you trying to make me feel different, even if you are trying to cheer me up."

"You're right. I'll shut up."

"So, I got depressed and starting really putting myself down. Here's the part that feels like a confession. I can't believe how embarrassed and naked I feel telling you this. I'm showing you my shame, David. I don't think I've ever done that before."

"I'm glad you are. I'm proud of you and feel a lot of love for you right now."

"Thanks. Okay, so I went to McDonald's and got a cheeseburger and fries and a milkshake. And I just scarfed it all down."

"That's it?"

"Yes, that's it. But that's terrible! I feel like I failed again."

"Yeah, I get it."

"But here's the one good part: It became absolutely clear like it never has been before that my emotional eating (which is comforting and punishing all at once) was a trance, or at least part of a trance. I mean, I could actually watch my feelings and thoughts and actions, and even my perception of myself, change like night and day. I can't say I am completely rid of the trance, but seeing it as a trance gives me a little peace and hope because I realize that this awful experience is contained in the trance that I can wake up from, like a bad dream. I can choose a different outcome if I can be fully present to myself!"

After a few weeks of sharing trances that were mostly neutral to their relationship, David and Ellen began including trances that involved each other. Following is an example of Ellen sharing and David listening.

"Last night when I came home from my meeting and found dirty dishes in the sink, I got really pissed. I was exhausted from such a long day and I knew you had taken the afternoon off. Since the dishes were still in the sink, I was sure you had been on your motorcycle all afternoon and had not bothered to take care of the few things at home I had asked you to help with. I was about to light into you for being so selfish and uncaring about what I need. But then I realized I had slipped into a trance and was making all kinds of assumptions that may not be true at all. Still, I wasn't able to come out of the trance at that point because my hurt and resentment were still running wild. So I decided to wait to bring this up now, when I'm not so activated."

A shared practice of awakening addresses the *context* of our relationships and will most definitely make problem solving much easier, less adversarial, more collaborative, and creative.

This would be a classic time for David to feel defensive, hurt, guilty, misjudged—who knows what else. If he reacts in a knee-jerk way, he might find a way to deflect or attack Ellen, or to defend or justify himself. But any of these reactions would indicate that David was in his own reactive trance, one in which he perceives that he is being attacked. Yet, Ellen is not attacking him at all. She is simply "reporting" from her practice of recognizing and observing her own trance state. Realizing that she was not yet able to shift while in the trance, Ellen chose wisely to not share that trance at the time. By waiting to communicate with David about her trance experience until she was no longer actively engaged in it, she is honoring her part of their parallel practice.

If David can remain in full present awareness, he will simply listen to Ellen's experience and respond to her in some way appropriate to the present moment. Perhaps he could express his appreciation that she waited until she was no longer entranced to share this with him. He could also share his own experience of the night before—perhaps even his own trance if he was in one. In any event, his response would not be defensive, or a justification of yesterday's actions, even if he thought he had a legitimate reason for not having done the dishes.

Couples often ask if their shared practice can be used to solve specific problems that arise in the course of their daily lives. They feel that they are creating a new forum for communicating about their practice of awakening, and that this could be an ideal opportunity to utilize the process for problem solving. My response is that while a shared practice will dramatically improve the nature and quality of our communication in general, it has a distinctly different purpose than solving specific problems. A shared practice of awakening addresses the *context* of our relationships and will most definitely make problem solving much easier, less adversarial, more collaborative, and creative. But attempting to blend them into the same conversation would dilute and compromise the practice of awakening. That said, separate and regular conversations to resolve specific issues and solve particular life problems are also vitally important.

A Parallel Practice: **Points to Remember**

The purpose of a parallel practice is to create a safe space (and process) where you and your partner are able to be vulnerable and transparent with each other with no need to defend or justify yourselves.

1. Establish a mutually agreed upon frequency, time, and place for the exclusive purpose of engaging in a parallel practice.
   - Once or twice a week seems best suited for most couples initially
   - A set amount of time, 45 min. to 1 hour for each meeting, is helpful
   - A time when neither are depleted or distracted
   - A place where both feel safe and secure

> **The nature and quality of our interpersonal experience will be markedly different, depending on the state of consciousness with which we identify within a given moment.**

2. Take turns sharing with each other the successes, challenges, and surprises of your ongoing individual practices.
   - Use this sharing to help fine-tune your skills of recognizing, observing, and shifting in relation to your own trances.
3. Listen to your partner's experience without critiquing, "helping," or teaching.
   - Questions for clarification and empathetic or congratulatory responses only!
4. Initially, talk only about those trances that do not directly involve your relationship.

At some point, having cultivated interpersonal trust in a *parallel practice,* we will feel ready to establish an *interactive practice*. It is important to keep in mind that while an interactive practice is powerful medicine if used wisely and lovingly, it can also be used as a manipulative tool or a hurtful weapon if we are still caught in our own trance issues. Therefore, if we have not fully developed the skills and the trust from a parallel practice, our interactive practice will likely land us in a quagmire of confusion, discord, and suffering.

Level Two: The Interactive Practice
An Introduction

So, exactly what is an *interactive practice* of awakening? Essentially, this is when both partners agree to use their relationship explicitly as a vehicle for quickening—their own and the other's—psychological awareness and spiritual awakening. In an interactive practice, we continue to utilize the three skills of *recognition, observation*, and *shifting*, and the sharing of what we have learned with our partner. But the focus is on the interactive trances that, over time, have become imbedded in our relationship.

Being creatures of habit, we tend to gravitate toward familiar patterns of thought, feeling, and interpersonal dynamics, and define our reality accordingly. The familiar patterns become part of our identity and create an implicit set of expectations, behaviors, rules, and obligations that get expressed in our relationship. When a couple becomes habituated to these interactive patterns, a private culture of two emerges, which becomes the *shared waking dream* of the relationship. The individuals of a couple relationship often will think, speak, and behave differently in situations outside the relationship. At work, social gatherings, or in solitude, other qualities, capabilities, moods, or areas of competence often will emerge. But when together, there is a strong tendency to re-enter the shared dream of their relationship where the familiar tone and quality of their interactions are resumed, re-enacted, and repeated.

> It is no surprise that so many relationships dissolve while fully engaged in the shared dream, without ever realizing it was a dream.

I am not suggesting that the couple relationship should be understood as *always* or *exclusively* occurring as a shared waking dream, any more than an individual is always or exclusively in a trance state. But virtually every couple manifests some degree of a shared waking dream at one time or another, given the natural propensity for entering trances in the first place. It is as if we have two distinct relationships with our partner: one that is rooted in the full present awareness of our awake selves, and one that is based on the trance identities of our shared waking dream. The nature and quality of our interpersonal experience will be markedly different, depending on the state of consciousness with which we identify within a given moment. This fact is neither bad nor unhealthy, in and of itself. It only becomes problematic when we suffer because we do not have an adequate understanding of what is occurring.

Suppose you and your partner have noticed that when you go to sleep at night, you each have a very active dream life. But rather than having a different dream each night, you each re-enter the same dream you had the night before. It is not exactly a recurring dream, because new and different things occur. It is more like a continuing dream that simply resumes each night when you go to sleep. As you talk about your dreams with each other, you make a remarkable discovery, which is that you have been entering the very same ongoing dream that your partner is having! Your perspectives of the dream are different, in that you each are dreaming from the point of view of your own identity. But the events and circumstances of the dream are the same. You are in each other's dream!

Now, let us suppose that there are certain elements of the dream that are not so pleasant. In fact, sometimes in this shared ongoing dream, the two of you become hurt or angry at one another. Or worse, you sustain long periods of time when both of you suffer, from arguments, from insecurities, feelings of betrayal, or resentments. Of course, when you wake up the next morning, the dream is gone. Whatever issues and problems you dreamt about last night belong to the dream reality, but not to your waking one. In your waking life, you and your partner love each other very deeply and are quite happy and at peace with your life together. The two realities are so different you might not even remember all of the problems of your dreams . . . until the next night when you go back to sleep. And, the problems resume every night when the dream continues, even after a wonderful, loving day spent with your partner.

> **It is our entrapment in the dream that temporarily defines us and denies us our freedom and joy.**

In the dream state, our interpersonal experience is based on needs, limitations, and fears that are created *by the dream*. Because our perceived needs can seem to compete with our partner's, the dream often has an adversarial quality—in which someone is right and someone is wrong, someone wins and someone loses, someone offends and someone is hurt. These differences are crucially important in our dream, and are sometimes irresolvable. It is no surprise that so many relationships dissolve while fully engaged in the shared dream, without ever realizing it was a dream.

By contrast, in our fully awake state, we understand that the adversarial polarities that seem so real in our dream are merely products of the dream, of which we are equal co-creators. We may even recognize some of these polarities as expressions of our complementary dysfunctional patterns, entwined together as part of the fabric of the dream. When we are awake and feeling our love for each other, the particular end of a polarity that we may represent in our dream matters very little. If anyone suffers, both suffer. From an awake perspective, it is clear that the culprit is always the trance or dream itself, never the particulars within it. It is our entrapment in the dream that temporarily defines us and denies us our freedom and joy.

But here it gets a bit trickier. In our analogy, the distinction between dreaming and being awake is clear because we have the condition of physical sleep to keep the two states of consciousness separate. But in our ordinary daily consciousness, there is no physically obvious distinction between being truly awake and being in a trance state or waking dream. Individually, we tend to slip in and out of trances almost seamlessly. In our relationships, being awake together and then spontaneously re-entering our shared waking dream often occurs instantaneously, with no notice.

To make matters more difficult, not only are we usually identified with only one of these relationships at a time—as each resides in a different state of consciousness—there is often a great disparity between the two relationships. The unfortunate irony in this complex is that in the reality of the waking dream, where our suffering is the greatest, and where the clarity and wisdom of our awake self is needed most, it is generally not accessible to us.

However, there is some good news. It is in exactly this place that our interactive practice can be so immensely helpful. While one person temporarily may be focused exclusively within the entranced aspect of the relationship, the other person might, in that same moment, have the benefit of full present awareness and be able to serve as a kind of *emissary* from their awake relationship. It is as if one of the partners could consciously travel from the awake state into the shared dream reality in order to bring the needed love, wisdom, and larger perspective. Another day, or another hour, the partners' roles might well be reversed. The principles and processes of the interactive practice are so vital to the well-being of our relationships that I am devoting the rest of this volume to its understanding and mastery.

CHAPTER SIX

6

An Interactive Practice Stage One: Preparation

Initially, an interactive practice can feel daunting because it is such a different approach to relationships than what most of us are familiar with. It may appear too complex to immediately grasp or too subtle to easily master. Yet, just as with our other practices, an interactive practice will seem natural and fluid, once we successfully experience it a few times and become more familiar with how it works. The final two chapters are devoted to helping couples establish a dependable step-by-step process that they can follow until they become comfortable enough, and gain enough experience, that they can adapt it to their own unique situation and needs.

There are two stages to an interactive practice: the preparation stage and the application stage. This chapter will explore the first stage, which consists of three steps:

- establish partnership of mutual intent
- identify parameters of shared trance states
- establish personalized "wake-up" cues

The second stage, *waking up inside the dream*, is the most challenging to both explain and to master, and will be examined in chapter 7.

Step One:
Establish Partnership of Mutual Intent

The first step is to establish a *partnership of mutual intent to awaken.* This step is the cornerstone of our practice and will serve as our primary frame of reference. This partnership is based on an agreement made while both are in full present awareness. Using the concept of lucid dreaming as a general framework, we enter an explicit agreement of deep and abiding intent to be equal partners committed to offering loving support and mutual assistance in waking up together within our shared waking dream.

This agreement contains two essential components. First, a genuine acceptance of personal responsibility for our own individual trances and, therefore, our own process of awakening. Integral to this process is our ongoing practice of consistently incorporating the three skills of *recognition, observation,* and *shifting.* Second, the understanding that our real and authentic relationship is between the beings we truly are, not the trance identities with whom we become entangled when in the dreamed aspects of our relationship.

To begin step one, each person must bring his or her attention fully to the present moment, as the present moment is the only moment in which we can have conscious awareness of our awake self or soul. This will tend to evoke a peaceful state of relaxed alertness. If this state is not immediately apparent, we can ask, "Am I, in this moment, awake?" We are checking to see if we are in a peaceful state of mind, free of any emotional reactivity, observant of our present internal and external experience, and feeling open-hearted. It is essential that both are present and awake in order to proceed with step one. Otherwise, the partnership will not be truly mutual. If we need to engage our individual practice in order to shift into this state, it is important that this be acknowledged openly and without judgment, and then followed through with before continuing this step.

Our real and authentic relationship is between the beings we truly are, not the trance identities with whom we become entangled.

When both are clearly in a present and awake state together, find a space to sit facing each other. Acknowledge your intent to know your partner and to be known by them at the level of your souls. Let your mind and heart attune to your clearest perception of, and feeling for, the sacred essence of your beloved. Let your eyes take your partner in, perhaps alternating between meeting their eyes, to letting your vision drift over and around their body. Observe how they are presenting themselves to you in this moment, and notice things, such as their posture, or the expression on their face, or their breathing, or any twitching or shifting of their weight.

As you continue to open and settle into a sense of your own deeper truth, you will become more able to behold your partner as the sacred being they truly are.

Notice any emotional reactions or judgments or opinions about your partner that may arise in you as you look at them. As you do this, gently acknowledge to yourself that these reactions, judgments, or opinions represent nothing more than aspects of your shared dream. They are completely entwined in the narrative level or story of the trance and are very seductive. Now is the time to remember that, whether subtle or obvious, fleeting or persistent, it is our reactions, judgments, and opinions that reinforce our primary identification with the dream and distract us from opening to our true awake self, our soul.

Knowing this, allow yourself to see beneath the surface level of your partner, beyond the narrative where all drama occurs. You may want to close your eyes at some point in order to feel their presence without any visual input. This is a wonderful opportunity to go deeper than your ordinary casual observation and interaction with your partner to discover something new or different about one another that perhaps you had not noticed or realized before.

As your heart opens more and more deeply, the layers of your partner's dreamed self will become progressively transparent. You may see traces or remnants of old emotional wounds, sorrows, or betrayals in the look of their eyes or in the way their shoulders slightly slump. In your mind's eye, allow the trances and the accumulated stories of their life to momentarily melt away. As you continue to open and settle into a sense of your own deeper truth, you will become more able to behold your partner as the sacred being they truly are. You will be able to appreciate their innate beauty, their innocence, and their vulnerability. You will be able to recognize the essential truth and goodness of their soul.

This is the time to acknowledge—to yourself and to your partner—your choice to share this sacred journey of awakening, in this time, in these bodies, in this life together. Now is the time to be utterly real, humble, and naked in your love for one another. It is the time to acknowledge your relationship as a partnership of souls, and to declare your mutual intent to offer and receive support and assistance in waking up together as you enter and re-enter the trances of your shared dream. Before you leave this space, anchor the experience in your hearts. It is the sacred space of your souls where you can return to at any time, together or alone, to remember who you are.

Key Points of Step One

1. Bring your attention fully to the present moment.
2. Acknowledge your intent to know and to be known by your partner at the level of your souls.
3. Take time together to sift through trance identifications, and the historical circumstances and issues of your personal stories, to discern and behold your deeper, truer selves in the present moment.
4. Acknowledge your own responsibility and personal commitment to continuing your individual practice of awakening, incorporating the skills of recognition, observation, and shifting.
5. Declare your mutual intent to offer and receive support and assistance in waking up together in a spirit of love, humility, and non-competition.

Step Two: Identify Parameters of Shared Trances

While both partners are awake and in full present awareness, *openly and honestly identify any ongoing or repeated shared trances* that have become a part of the relationship. This includes any dysfunctional patterns that have become incorporated into the basic repertoire of repeated arguments, historical issues, or other sore spots that keep being re-lived or re-hashed in the relationship. This could also include familiar tones and textures of repeated interactions, or long-sustained moods that seem specific to the relationship. One of the telltale signs of a couple engaged in their shared waking dream is when either partner has a feeling of "here we go, again." This feeling usually indicates a pattern that has grown to define some aspect of the relationship. All of these elements combined will begin to define the parameters of the shared waking dreams of the relationship and to distinguish them from the original and spontaneous moments that occur when each person is in full present awareness.

It is helpful to be explicit and detailed when we identify the areas and parameters of our shared trance states. Naming a particular trance—such as our *traveling* trance; our *money-spending argument* trance; our *sex* trance; or our *house chores* trance—helps to identify it. Naming each trance will also help to objectify and externalize the pattern as a separate entity. This will make it easier to recognize and observe our experience with less emotional attachment when we find ourselves in the trance at a later time.

> **One of the telltale signs of a couple engaged in their shared waking dream is when either partner has a feeling of "here we go, again."**

Once a trance has been identified and named, it is helpful to map out the habitual sequence of the interactive pattern. For instance, what sets it in motion, who says what, and where it usually leads. As we discuss our patterns, we can each identify our own role in the trance, including the primary emotional reactions that we typically get hooked into at the time. We should only speak for ourselves, and refrain from analyzing our partner's reactivity. It is generally helpful to compile a written list of all our shared trances. Some prefer to create a visual model as well, by drawing an outline of all the trances on a large sheet of paper, and then labeling each trance and noting each other's primary role.

Inevitably, some trances will be more emotionally charged than others. Those trances that are rooted in deep, traumatic, or primitive childhood wounds are likely to be more challenging to identify without being drawn into the old pain. For this reason, I recommend that after initially listing all the shared trances that come to mind, you earmark those that feel the scariest to address later, and start with those trances that do not feel as emotionally risky. Getting your feet wet with lighter trances should give you more practice and confidence as you progress toward the more challenging trances.

It is appropriate to express our feelings or concerns about our trance or dream experiences while we are doing step two. But it is important to remember that the purpose of this step is to identify the shared waking dream *as a trance state*, not as Truth, and to do so from a present and awake perspective. Therefore, even though we may be concerned about the dream as a whole, we will be speaking from the observer's perspective, without a strong attachment to our role in the dream. To get the gist of this, let's listen in on a step-two conversation between Jessie and Patrick as they learn this practice.

"Patrick, I've been thinking about our relationship and looking for times when we get into our old trances together," Jessie begins, one morning sitting up in bed, having a cup of coffee.

"Any luck?"

"Yeah, I think so. But is this an okay time for you, for us to talk about it?"

"I've got some time before I need to get up. And I'm feeling pretty open this morning. So, sure. What did you come up with?"

"Well, first, I want to check in with myself to be sure I am fully present and aware. The trance I think I have identified makes me anxious."

"Oh yeah," I guess I should do that, too."

"Okay," Jessie says, sighing faintly, "I'm pretty grounded. How about you?"

"I'm feeling pretty calm, warm," Patrick responds, nodding thoughtfully. "Yep. I feel centered, good, ready to go."

"Well, I think our argument yesterday would definitely qualify as a trance."

"You mean about your mother coming to stay with us this summer?"

"Yes."

"It did get pretty nasty, didn't it? I've gotta tell you, Jessie, I still don't know what happened. I really don't understand why you got so mad."

"I don't think I understood at the time either. But you know, at one point I just wanted to scream at you and shake you."

"Oh, I know. I felt it. It was kind of freaky at first. I didn't think I had done anything to get you so mad. I was only talking about how I would have to change my schedule if your mother came. And then all hell broke loose!"

"I can kind of see that now. But it sure didn't seem that way yesterday. You know Mom is a painful topic for me any

time. And yesterday, when you were talking, it felt like you had no interest in supporting my relationship with her. I felt so hurt and mad at you. And completely justified in blaming you."

"But I really don't feel that way, Jessie. I want you and your mom to heal your relationship. And if we worked out the details, it would probably be fine for her to visit this summer."

While the trance Jessie and Patrick are identifying occurred yesterday, their actual relationship is occurring now, in the present moment. Notice how Patrick has just spoken about his true feelings in the present moment, rather than defending or rehashing what he said yesterday. This might well provide Jessie with new information about Patrick, distinct from what she perceived in their shared trance. Remember, the purpose of Step two is simply to identify the various trances and their parameters, not try to resolve specific issues within them. But sometimes a comment about what we feel or believe in our awake state can provide helpful clarification.

"You really mean that don't you, Patrick?"

"Yes, I really do."

"So why were you such an ass?"

"Well, if you remember, I didn't start out that way. I was just trying to figure out how we could pull it off, and how I would need to rearrange my schedule in order to refinish the floor in the guest bathroom. You know, I had planned to do that in the fall, but if your mother came in the summer, my original plan wouldn't work. Then, when you assumed I was being resistant, and started talking to me in a mean tone of voice and telling me I wasn't honoring your relationship, I felt surprised and hurt. And when you wouldn't let up, I got mad because I felt so misunderstood and unappreciated. By then, my old trance of feeling trapped and resentful took over, just like in the past. At that point, I have to admit, I was an ass. And, just like you, I felt totally justified."

"Oh, so that was it." Jessie reviews the scene in her mind. "I knew I had touched a raw nerve because, all of a sudden, you got right in my face."

"I definitely had a knee-jerk reaction."

"Okay, I get it," Jessie replies thoughtfully. "So we were off and running, both in our trances, as usual."

"Exactly. Both of us were feeling hurt and angry, and both of us were feeling totally justified in our righteous indignation. Right there is our waking dream, isn't it?"

"It's certainly part of it. I sure don't feel any of that when we are fully present, like now."

"No, me neither."

"Its such a shame, Patrick. If only we could remember who we really are, you know, like who we are with each other right now."

"While we were in the midst of our dream?"

"Well, yeah!"

"But Jessie, I still feel like I'm just learning how to make that happen! I mean, when I am in the dream, I feel so totally defined by it, there doesn't seem to be any break, any opening even to clue me in to the fact that I am dreaming."

This practice is not about demanding perfection; it is about waking up as soon as we are able.

"But we have been catching ourselves some. And it feels so cool when we do."

"True enough. So, what other trances do we share?"

This confessional conversation is equivalent to recognizing the trance after the fact. But it is more than that. Jessie and Patrick are also sharing their mutual lament about their suffering when they get caught in their dream. By sharing their experience with honesty and humility, they are nurturing a feeling of genuine partnership based on the love, honor, and mutuality which is inherent in the present moment of their awake relationship. This kind of relationship, rooted in both partner's awake state, is the foundation of an interactive practice.

If, at any time during such a conversation, we feel ourselves slipping into a reactive trance, it is vital that we stop for a moment, breath, bring our careful attention back to our present state, call on our skills of observation, and remind ourselves that we are doing step two of our practice. In other words, we must make sure that we are staying awake and still feeling connected to each other in our practice so that our conversation does not draw us back into the very dream we are attempting to identify. If this occurs, and we are not able in that moment to reconnect in our awake state, it is preferable to simply own up to being in our own trance, apologize, and postpone our conversation until we are fully awake.

This practice will strengthen and deepen as we continue to work at it. We do not need to be hard on ourselves, nor our partner, for slipping into a trance when first learning this process. It will happen to most of us at one time or another. This practice is not about demanding perfection; it is about waking up as soon as we are able. Ironically, judging ourselves, or our partner, for not being always awake is an action that further entraps us in our trance state, or dream.

Key Points of Step Two

1. Together, identify, name, and list all ongoing or repeated shared trances.
2. Earmark the more emotionally charged or challenging trances, and start mapping the parameters of the less "risky" trances first in order to build more skill and confidence before progressing to the more challenging trances.
3. Map out the parameters of each trance, including:
   a. the triggering event or circumstance
   b. the sequence and style of the interaction
   c. each partner's role in the trance
   d. the primary emotional qualities and reactions of each role

Step Three: Establish Personalized "Wake Up" Cues

We have looked at the one central question that sets in motion our practice of awakening: "Am I, in this moment, awake?" But what if we are so immersed in our trance, or waking dream, that it does not even occur to us to ask the question? Or what if we happen to be awake and notice that our beloved partner is caught in a trance but does not realize it? Inevitably, there will be times when our awake and dreaming states will not be in sync with our partner, and it will be these times when a gesture of loving assistance to or from our partner will hold much value.

The most helpful assistance needed at these times is a compassionate reminder or friendly "wake up" nudge. A nudge that reminds us to ask ourselves if we are awake. Anything more generally will not be helpful as it will place too much emphasis on the contents of the dream and will likely invite resistance.

A variation of our bedroom analogy can serve to further illustrate this point. Let us say you and your partner are in bed one evening. Your partner is sound asleep but you are not tired and are sitting up in bed reading a favorite book in the soft light of your bedside lamp. It is a warm summer night and there is a gentle rain falling lightly on the roof and nearby trees. The air smells fresh, your bed is very comfortable, your breathing is relaxed, and you feel a deep sense of peace and well-being. You glance over at your partner and feel such love and appreciation for this person in your life. But you notice that they are fitful in their sleep.

As you watch your beloved more closely, it becomes clear that they are agitated and appear to be having a disturbing dream. You know that they are in bed, safe and sound, even if they are dreaming that they are somewhere else, struggling or in danger. You know that their suffering is something they are dreaming and that they do not need to be "fixed" or "rescued." But they do seem to be trapped in a painful dream. So, out of simple love and compassion, you reach over and gently nudge your partner. As they give you a groggy half-response, you lean close to their ear and whisper, "You looked like you were having a bad dream. Are you okay?"

That, in essence, is all you do. What your partner does with your nudge is up to your partner. They might wake up, or they might roll over and go back to sleep. They may or may not resume their dream. What you offered from an awake consciousness was enough of a break in the momentum of their dream to rouse their attention and give them a moment of choice. It is this same moment of choice that we are attempting to achieve in

There will be times when our awake and dreaming states will not be in sync with our partner, and it will be these times when a gesture of loving assistance to or from our partner will hold much value.

our interactive practice. For whoever happens to be awake to offer a gentle "wake up" nudge intended to create a momentary break in the momentum of our partner's dreaming. The degree to which they have cultivated the intent to be awake will be reflected in what they do next, a choice that must be entirely their own.

Yet, to provide even a friendly nudge is not always simple because the one who is still dreaming will have the tendency to interpret the assistance through the lens of the dream/trance. What may be intended as a helpful reminder may be interpreted as a judgment or a challenge or an invalidating comment by the one still dreaming. This is much like when we are asleep and dreaming and the phone rings. The sound of the ring will often be reinterpreted and incorporated into something happening in the dream, something other than simply an actual telephone ring.

> If we feel a need to offer more than a nudge, it is likely that we are operating from our own trance state.

To minimize the likelihood that a wake up nudge is misinterpreted, it is critically important that each chooses the particular way assistance is to be offered. That way, we will recognize and receive the nudge in the spirit of the awake agreement, even while in the midst of our dream. This requires personal reflection and perhaps some searching for just the right wake-up cue, one that really clicks for us. Once each person thinks they have identified the cue (or code or key) that will work for them while in the dream, we are to share this with our partner. It is important to provide specific words or a phrase and tie this to a gesture or tone of voice that we know we would immediately recognize as a friendly wake-up nudge. The language or gesture may or may not be the same for both. Either way, it is essential that the person, anticipating their need to wake up, be the one who determines what and how their reminder is offered.

For this process to succeed, it is equally essential that when we are the one offering assistance, we follow precisely the instructions of our partner by using their specific words, tone of voice, etc. Once the cue has been tentatively established, it is a good idea to repeat it back a few times. This allows the one choosing their own cue to "try it on" and make any adjustments that might be needed to assure the right fit. As the one being taught our partner's cue, we must honor the fact that we are being given the "inside scoop" on how we can get through to them, a key which they will be cued to recognize. This is one time when explicitly following directions without questioning them is much more effective that any improvisation. Help that cannot be received is no help at all, and the point is to offer a wake-up nudge that can be received as such, and genuinely welcomed. Therefore, it is important to write down our partner's exact comment and then make sure we follow it precisely.

It is also essential that the one being given this key make a firm commitment not to use it unless we are awake ourselves. If we feel a need to offer more than a nudge, it is likely that we are operating from our own trance state. One way to be sure that we are awake enough to offer a wake-up nudge is to be clear that there are no emotional demands attached to our offer. In other words, before we ever offer a wake-up nudge to our partner, we need to give them complete permission (in our heart) not to receive or be ready to act upon our nudge.

Key Points of Step Three

1. Each partner chooses a comment, phrase, or question to serve as a personalized wake-up cue.
2. Each shares the exact words, tone of voice, and gestures (if relevant) that would most likely and readily be received as a friendly, non-challenging, wake-up nudge.
3. Each repeats back exact words, tone of voice, and gestures (if any) and tweak as necessary until it feels just right to our partner.
4. Each partner writes down exact comment (for safe-keeping and later reference) and agrees not to change or improvise when using.
5. Both promise to offer a wake-up nudge only in a spirit of compassion, humility, and non-attachment to our partner's response (i.e., never while we are in a trance state).
6. Both promise that when our partner offers us our wake-up nudge, we will do our very best to honor our agreement to receive it in the spirit in which it is being offered.

CHAPTER SEVEN

An Interactive Practice Stage Two: Application

Waking Up Inside the Dream

All three steps of stage one occur while we are in a fully present and awake state. These steps represent the preparatory aspects of an interactive practice of awakening by establishing mutual intent, defining the parameters of our shared trances, and creating an effective strategy using "wake-up" cues. Stage two, waking up inside the dream, occurs within the entranced realm of our shared waking dream, and it is to this arena where our practice directs its attention, and where our preparation and our intent ultimately will be tested. It is also where our individual skills of recognition, observation, and shifting truly pay off. Just as if we were asleep and dreaming, our shared waking dream is where we actually learn to lucid dream, where theory becomes experience.

Stage two is uniquely challenging for one obvious reason. While we may select a designated time and place to do each step of stage one, stage two occurs spontaneously in the trenches of our ongoing life, and is just as likely to be initiated by our partner as by ourselves. Just as circumstances and personal issues will vary in degree of importance and intensity, our own and our partner's energy, mental clarity, and emotional availability will be different at different times. Our success with this stage will depend on our ability to remember who we are and what we agreed to when we were awake.

Learning to master this stage is like learning to drive a car. The principles and skills of driving remain consistent, but how we apply them depends on many variables, such as the type and condition of the road, weather conditions, visibility, the flow of traffic, etc. Similarly, the principles and skills of waking up inside the dream of our relationship are consistent. But the practice of applying them must be developed as we live our lives. This will require, among other skills, flexibility and adaptability.

Of course, our knowledge and skill will have to be practiced and honed through experience. We will make mistakes and botch our attempts several times before we master this step. But, like any true psychological growth or spiritual practice, if we keep heart and persevere, it does begin to get easier and to feel more natural. I have interspersed a few examples in this section to illustrate the variety of situations where the principles of an interactive practice could be applied.

This stage requires our willingness to be both active and receptive. At any given moment, it could be us or it could be our partner who is either awake or fully entranced. For the one who is awake, the idea is to use our partner's cue, precisely as instructed, and offer it to them as a friendly "wake-up" nudge. For the one who is, at the moment, fully identified with the dream, their responsibility is to acknowledge and receive the cue offered by their partner, which, while in our awake state, we both agreed to honor at just such a moment as this.

This stage requires our willingness to be both active and receptive. At any given moment, it could be us or it could be our partner who is either awake or fully entranced.

When the wake-up nudge is offered and received, the momentum of the dream will be interrupted. If the one receiving the nudge is able to shift and fully access their awake self, then a simple acknowledgment of the shift will be all that is needed. The one who has just become conscious of their dreaming might wish to thank their partner for their willingness to risk offering the reminder, knowing their own potential to stay in their trance and get defensive. Likewise, the one who offered the reminder might thank the one who allowed the wake-up nudge to get their attention for honoring their practice in such a challenging moment. These acknowledgments can serve to encourage each of us and to reaffirm our commitment to continue this practice, which, at least in the beginning, will not always go so smoothly. Otherwise, we are then free to continue or discontinue whatever else we were engaged in, depending on our choice at the time.

If both happen to be fully engaged in a shared dream, and one partner begins to wake up on their own, that person needs to acknowledge the discovery of their own trance only. If the shared dream is taking place during an intense or painful moment, such as in the midst of an argument, the one who is waking up should simply state that, given their own trance, they wish to disengage in the interaction until they are fully awake and can approach the difficulty from a more centered, loving, and honoring place.

It is essential that we honor the agreement to return to the conversation when we are both awake.

This initial "confession" may or may not be enough to cue their partner about their own entrancement. It should at least interrupt the momentum of their dreamed reality. If it does, and both partners are able to immediately acknowledge their practice of awakening and access their feelings of loving partnership, they may choose to continue their interaction. This would create an ideal opportunity to talk about their current trance experience (but now from their awake/observer self) and begin to *experience the exquisite beauty and relief of waking up together.*

It is also quite possible that our partner will need more time. And, just as we begin to wake up, we may still be identified enough with the trance that we could easily slip back into it with the slightest bit of provocation. Both of these possibilities must be honored. If either does not feel confident, both to be in our dream and in our awake partnership simultaneously, then the most appropriate action is to temporarily disengage from the trance interaction with a verbal agreement to return to the conversation after we have had time to reconnect with our awake self. Such a choice, when genuinely agreed upon, is itself a movement toward waking up together.

It is essential that we honor the agreement to return to the conversation when we are both awake. We can use the same shared sacred space already established in our parallel practice as we include this recent experience as further identification of the parameters of our shared waking dream (stage two) and begin to talk about our experience from the perspective of our awake self. Coming back to our difficult experience, but now as partners who are humbly learning about waking up (acknowledging but not identifying with our adversarial roles in the dream), both strengthens our partnership and reaffirms our commitment to our path of awakening.

Consider the following example of Lucy and Greg, both in their mid-30s and married for almost three years. They have been engaged in a shared practice of awakening for just a few months.

Recently, Lucy and Greg were overjoyed to learn that Lucy was pregnant. They decided to create a meditation garden as a symbolic way to prepare for the arrival of their new child, and to plant a rosebush in the center of the garden as a symbol of the love and beauty of their already cherished child. For the past two weeks, when one or both of them had time, they worked on the garden. Everything seemed to be going well; they chose the perfect spot for the rosebush, then cleared the weeds and rocks, prepared the soil, until the day finally arrived that they planned to plant the shrub.

It was a hotter-than-usual late-spring Sunday afternoon. A couple of days earlier, Greg had broken out with a bad case of poison ivy and had not been able to sleep. He started out irritable and became even more agitated as he kept hitting roots with his shovel while trying to dig a deep enough hole for the rosebush. After giving up on the first two attempts, Greg was on his third hole. On top of that, as he worked and sweated, his poison ivy itched more intensely.

Lucy had had an argument with her mother that morning about her plans to have a natural childbirth with the assistance of a midwife. Her mother was adamantly opposed to this plan. Lucy felt criticized and bullied in the conversation, and was still angry at her mother when she joined Greg in the garden. He had been digging unsuccessfully for about forty-five minutes before Lucy joined him, rosebush in hand.

"Why are you digging a hole there?" Lucy began, "I thought we agreed to put the rosebush in the center."

"There are too many roots there."

"But we planned the whole garden around the center spot!" Lucy lamented.

"I know."

"Can't you just cut the roots with your shovel?"

"No. I tried. There are too many and they are hard as a rock," Greg answered abruptly, as a bead of sweat rolled down his face. He tried to wipe it away with his shirtsleeve, but a speck of dirt got in his eye.

"What about over there?" Lucy asked, pointing to Greg's second unsuccessful spot, which he had subsequently smoothed back over. "I like that spot better than the one you picked here."

"I already tried there," Greg answered dismissively as he squinted, attempting to remove the dirt from his eye.

"There?" she said as she pointed to the same spot.

"Yes, dammit, there!"

"Hey, you don't have to be so pissy!"

"Well, if you don't like the way I dig, or where I put the hole, then here—you take the shovel and do it better!"

"I was just asking."

"No, you were complaining. And I've been out here for almost an hour just trying to dig a friggin' hole!"

Lucy didn't immediately respond. She was surprised at Greg's short temper and felt her own anger still lingering from her argument with her mother. After a few more minutes of shoveling, Greg thought he had managed to dig the third hole deep enough. "Would you hand me the bush?" he said with a thinly veiled sneer.

The bush was not very large, about three feet high, including the roots, but was an awkward shape with several canes already growing in odd directions. Greg was kneeling by the hole as he reached out to get the bush from Lucy. He thought he had judged where the thorns were but stuck himself anyway. He cursed and reflexively jerked his hand back. As he did this, he bumped one of the canes with his arm and snatched the rosebush out of Lucy's hand, slicing her finger with a thorn in the process.

"Ouch! Dammit, Greg!"

"What?"

"What!? You just jerked the bush out of my hand and cut me! What is your problem?"

Lucy felt ready to chew him out if he said even one wrong word. That readiness, perhaps even a flash of desire to fight him, was what got her attention enough to remember her practice. She had been experimenting with asking herself at random moments, "Am I, in this moment, awake?" But this time she didn't actually need to ask and answer. Her trance was self-evident the moment the question even arose. What she did say to herself was, "I am definitely in a trance right now." The power of this awareness was stunning. She just put her hands up and shook her head slightly. "You know, Greg, I just realized I am in a trance right now. And I don't think anything I could say at this moment would be helpful. I don't know what's going on with you, but I want to honor our agreement. So I need to be alone for a while until I can get centered in myself."

Lucy's comment facilitated the break in momentum that Greg hadn't been able to create for himself. Greg came out of the fog of his trance just enough to acknowledge that he was also in one. "That's probably a good idea. I'm in a foul mood. And I can't seem to get out of it. So, I guess there's my trance, too."

"Let's talk later, okay?"
"Okay."

Later that evening, recovered from their trance episode, Lucy and Greg went for a walk to talk about their experience.

"This afternoon was amazing," Lucy began, "I was so mad at Mom before I even brought the rosebush out to you. And I don't know what was up with you, but all it took was a couple of nasty comments, and I was ready to tear your head off."

"Well, I should have warned you that it wasn't a good time to approach me. If I had had more presence of mind, I probably would have known that I shouldn't have even been outside. My poison ivy was making me want to crawl out of my skin it itched so bad. I haven't slept well for two days, and the ground I was digging was unbelievably hard. I was fit to be tied before you ever came outside. And then when you didn't like where I was digging, as if I wanted to be digging there in the first place, it just pushed me over the edge."

"I had no idea, Greg. I'm so sorry."

"Well, how could you have known all that? I was too caught up in it to even tell you. But thanks for being aware enough to see where we were headed and to name our trance."

"Hey, I was just trying to wake up from my trance because it felt so crappy!"

"It helped me, too."

"I'm glad."

"So, why were you so mad at your mom?"

Lucy's recognition of her trance, and her clear and simple statement to honor their agreement, was enough to cue Greg. Had she chosen to address Greg's trance, instead, the situation would likely have degenerated into further blame and defensiveness. As it was, they were able to come back together and talk about their individual trances and how each interacted with the other's trance. This particular incident was not one that they had initially identified. In hindsight, they realized that they both had felt distressed before they ever interacted. Greg now included physical distress as a potential trance trigger for himself. This incident also alerted Lucy and Greg to the anxiety they felt—along with the joy—about having a child. This prompted them to identify anxiety, and other fear-based reactions, related to their anticipation of having a child as a potential area of their shared dream.

But what if one of us is so embedded in our dream, so intensely fused with it that we are not able, in that moment, to recognize it or even to acknowledge a wake-up nudge, much less to shift our consciousness? This is when the one who offered the nudge must remember that their beloved partner is temporarily trapped in a contracted and suffering dream. Remember, they are the one suffering, not you. They would not choose to be in an unhappy dream if they truly realized they had a choice. That very realization is the whole point of this practice! They simply have not mastered it yet, just like at other times, when we have been, or will be, caught in our dream.

It may be that in that moment, we are the only one who is able to hold the vision and the space of our awake relationship. To do that is a true act of love and is not even difficult if we can stay awake as the moment unfolds. *Learning to stay awake when our beloved partner is not able to join us in that state is as important a part of this practice as learning to wake up when we are the one caught in the dream.* If we can remain awake, we will be able to have compassion for our partner's trapped condition without taking their dream personally (even if a negative image of us happens to be part of their dream).

From our awake state, we can acknowledge our partner's feelings and perceptions, and perhaps even empathize with them. But at the same time, we must not engage in the dynamics of the dream itself. For instance, we would clearly refrain from any polarized interaction, such as questioning, challenging, refuting or disagreeing with any aspect of our partner's dream content. Staying awake includes remembering that our primary relationship is with the person that our partner truly is, not the contracted trance identity with which they have temporarily fused.

> *Learning to stay awake when our beloved partner is not able to join us in that state is as important a part of this practice as learning to wake up when we are the one caught in the dream.*

Let's take one more look at Jessie and Patrick, this time as they demonstrate the skill and clarity they have learned after several months of integrating this practice into their daily lives. By now, they have gleaned a great deal from their individual trances, as well as their shared waking dream. They each have experienced being the one who wakes up first, as well as being the one caught in their dream long after the other has awakened. But because of their genuine commitment to their practice, they have generally been able to wake up together, sooner or later, from their entranced moments. The frequency of their painful shared trances is less now than when they began their practice but, more significant than that is the way they handle the trances when they do occur.

One morning, Jessie, Patrick, and Sara were hurrying to get ready for school and work when Jessie overheard part of a conversation between Patrick and Sara. Jessie was in another room but from what she heard, Patrick's words and tone of voice sounded accusatory toward Sara, and potentially shaming of her. In a surge of feeling protective of Sara, Jessie interrupted the conversation, saying to Patrick in a strong tone of voice, "Don't talk to her like that. She didn't do anything wrong!" Patrick was taken aback at first, but almost immediately got angry at Jessie's comment.

He finished his brief conversation with Sara and then went into the other room to confront Jessie. An intense flare of words and feelings ensued for a few moments as Jessie expressed her strong opinion that Patrick's communication with Sara sounded shaming. Patrick responded that he had not intended to shame Sara, and did not perceive that he had, nor did he perceive that Sara had felt shamed. On this point, they simply disagreed. But beyond that, Patrick said, emphatically and angrily, that regardless of whose perception about the shaming was correct, Jessie's way of interrupting and "correcting" him was disrespectful of him and his relationship with Sara, and was unacceptable. Jessie was angry, as well, and felt hurt by Patrick's comments. All of this took place in less than five minutes; their conversation got cut short because everyone was late. It wasn't until that evening that Patrick and Jessie had a chance to reconnect.

On their way to school, Patrick told Sara that Jessie was concerned that she might have felt shamed by him earlier that morning and, if that was true, he had not intended for it to come across that way and was very sorry. Sara was surprised by this comment and said that she had not felt shamed at all. To the contrary, she had interpreted Jessie's comment to be nothing more than the typical playful banter that the three of them engaged in fairly often. Feeling relieved that Sara was not hurt, Patrick relaxed enough to reflect upon what had happened and why he felt so incensed about it.

He remembered occasions in his previous marriage when his wife would interrupt his attempts to discipline the children (hers from a previous marriage) by defending them and challenging him in front of them, making him appear uncaring or unfair, rather than acknowledging and supporting his intention to be helpful. Those interactions had degenerated into painful, angry arguments that had frustrated and deeply hurt Patrick. The current situation was nowhere near the intensity of the past, nor were the dynamics the same. But there was enough similarity to activate some of the old pain. It was becoming clear to Patrick that at least some of the intensity of his pain and resentment that had erupted did not really belong to this morning. In fact, it was the instantaneous intensity of the pain which alerted him to the understanding that he had entered an old trance the moment Jessie made her initial comment.

This admission to himself felt tricky because he still held firmly to his opinion that the interruption was inappropriate, and did not want to dismiss that simply because he was also entranced emotionally. Simply acknowledging both aspects without negating either one of them allowed Patrick to become less defensive and less resentful, thus loosening the grip of the trance. As he gradually shifted from his trance identity to his awake (observer) self, he was able to imagine what it might have felt like to be on Jessie's end of the morning's interaction. He was also able to reconnect with how grateful he truly felt that Jessie cared enough about Sara's self-esteem to be willing to fight for her.

By the time Patrick arrived home that night, he was feeling warm and open to Jessie and was hoping that she had been able to sort out this morning for herself. But that was not the case. Jessie was quiet and kept to herself, and it was not until Patrick approached her and tried to engage her that he began to realize the extent and depth of her pain.

"How are you doing?" he began.
"Not good."

Patrick did not respond verbally. He sat down beside Jessie and remained quiet in order to give Jessie time to say more.

"What happened this morning was not okay," she began.
"No, it's not okay with me, either. I did speak to Sara on the way to school, and she said that she didn't feel shamed at all. She was very clear about that."
"I'm glad. But I'm not talking about that. The way you spoke to me felt so bad that I seriously thought about moving out today," Jessie said without looking at Patrick. "A part of me really wanted to just leave and disappear."

Patrick was surprised by this statement and responded with a look of puzzlement.

"You have no idea how much you hurt me this morning, Patrick. This is normally when I would leave a relationship."

Unlike other times, this evening Patrick did not feel defensive or alarmed. His trance of the morning had completely dissipated, and now he was left with love and appreciation for Jessie, and a great deal of compassion for her pain. Her statement about considering leaving him (knowing how much she loved him) was so out of proportion to his perception of what had occurred that morning, it made it clear to him that Jessie was in a very painful trance.

"Jessie, I know we both felt hurt and angry this morning and, you are right, I don't know how I hurt you so deeply. I do know that I love you deeply and I am sorry you are hurting."

"You falsely accused me of interfering with you every time you are confronting Sara," Jessie said, beginning to pace, "And that's just not true. I have held my tongue on other occasions when I didn't agree with how you were handling her because I know that's an issue with you. I know this morning I shouldn't have said anything, but I was just being concerned for your daughter!" Jessie began to cry. "There is nothing you could have said to me that would have been more hurtful."

"I don't even remember saying that."

"Well, you did. And it was untrue and unfair, and there is nothing more hurtful to me than being accused of something I didn't do." As Jessie said this she sat down and looked away from Patrick.

Patrick did not remember saying that Jessie interfered every time he confronted Sara. It was not his perception then or now that she interfered every time he confronted Sara. So he was puzzled that something he did not remember saying and did not even believe about her had triggered so much pain. His first impulse was to "correct" Jessie's perception about what he had said. But the depth of her pain indicated to him that such an approach would likely degenerate into an argument, which would not be helpful. Also, her extreme reaction—considering moving out of the house—was so incongruous with the nature and quality of the rest of their relationship, it was clear that Jessie was in a very contracted and suffering trance.

Patrick also was not certain of exactly what he had said. Maybe he had said those words but meant something else. Given his pain at the time, he realized it was quite possible that he had not been skillful in the way he had spoken. Or maybe he said something that was close to what she heard, but with a meaning different than the one she understood through the filter of her painful trance. He did not really know.

But what he had learned from their practice of awakening is that the specific contents of the dream are not what matters when we are awake, even though it sure seems to matter when we are fully entranced. So, what would be the point of engaging in a power struggle with Jessie? How could either one of them possibly benefit from that! What did matter to Patrick was that he stay awake and in his loving heart in this moment, remembering his agreement to do their practice, and to respond to Jessie from that context.

The specific contents of the dream are not what matters when we are awake, even though it sure seems to matter when we are fully entranced.

Notice, as our example continues, how Patrick stays in the present and speaks his truth without the adversarial quality of the trance. He neither concedes his own reality to Jessie's, nor does he try to refute her experience.

"Jessie, I can see how hurt you are and I am truly sorry. I know you haven't interfered every time I have confronted Sara. I never thought that you had. So I am really surprised that that is what you remember me saying. But maybe I was speaking from my own trance and, in my own frustration, I misspoke. I honestly don't know. But if there is anything I don't want to do, it is to hurt you by unfairly accusing you of something. I am very grateful that you care enough to stand up for Sara when you think she needs it. She is blessed to have you in her corner."

At that point, Patrick reached over to gently touch Jessie's cheek and to make eye contact with her. She recoiled slightly and kept looking away. The wake-up nudge that Jessie had given Patrick was to look her in the eyes and say in a gentle, reassuring tone of voice, "Hey, I'm loving you right now," with the promise that he would never say it unless he was truly feeling it. Since Jessie could not allow him that eye contact just yet, now was not the time to offer her a wake-up nudge. This did not disturb Patrick.

Since he had managed to stay awake during this interaction, he was able to see his beloved Jessie caught in a very painful dream that she just hadn't been able to pull herself out of yet. He was seeing her and believing in her in this very moment of her dream, knowing there was only a thin veil of consciousness that kept her trapped in it. So, in a feeling of tenderness and genuine support, he responded, "You're pulling away so I guess you don't want to connect with me, yet. Do you need more time to be alone?"

"Did I pull away? I didn't realize."

"Yeah, just then. But that's okay, I just don't want to crowd you. Do you want me to give you some space?"

"Maybe. I don't know. I am glad that you sought me out this evening." As Jessie said this, she looked Patrick in the eyes.

This gave Patrick the opening he was waiting for. "Hey, I'm loving you right now."

Jessie sighed and waited for a moment before she responded, "I know you do. I do need to be alone for a while, though. I may go to bed soon."

"Okay, that's fine," Patrick said as he got up to leave. "You know, this is not about us."

"Yeah, I know. I'm realizing that the depth of this pain is clearly beyond our relationship. Will you kiss me before you go?"

Patrick kissed her. "I hope you sleep well. You look exhausted."

"I am exhausted. Thank you for talking to me."

We can see that, once awakened from his trance, Patrick was able to remain awake when he re-engaged with Jessie. Jessie had had the day to simmer in and reflect upon her trance, but had not yet awakened from it. Had Patrick attempted to interact before he was awake, his agenda would have been to promote or defend his position, and the conversation would likely have degenerated into simply another round of the fight. But since his shift was genuine, there was no contentious or adversarial quality about him that certainly would have agitated the emotional energy which Jessie was attempting to manage. Therefore, it did not take long for Jessie to trust him and become receptive to his responses to her. Her comment to Patrick that she realized the depth of her pain was "beyond our relationship" shows that she had *recognized* and was *observing* her trance, even though she had not fully *shifted* yet. But even that much awareness allowed them to respectfully create some space to be alone, which set the stage for later, when both of them could share their experience of the dream as loving partners learning how to wake up together.

But suppose the situation is more extreme and one partner is not willing or able to honor the other's request to disengage. If, after repeating the request clearly and simply a few times, our partner refuses to acknowledge our request to disengage, then we are not engaged in a shared practice of awakening at that time. It may be that the best thing we can do is to give our partner physical and emotional space to stay in their trance. This may simply mean leaving the room. If that is not enough, we may need to go for a walk, or run some errands, or do anything that temporarily creates some distance.

It is imperative that we never use withdrawal with any intent to hurt or control our partner.

This is not something we would negotiate with our partner. If our partner cannot honor our request to disengage, then our attempts to negotiate would likely degenerate into an argument or power struggle. Rather, it is a time to accept that we are the only one we can be in charge of, and act compassionately but decisively according to our own perceptions of what is needed. It is important to keep in mind that withdrawal is a powerful action that also can be used toxically as punishment and/or manipulation. Clearly, this can evoke strong negative reactions. Therefore, it is imperative that we never use withdrawal with any intent to hurt or control our partner.

Later, when both partners are in an awake state, we will likely need to revisit the first three steps of our interactive practice and try to determine what it was that made this dream so dominating and waking up so challenging. This will not be one person pointing the finger at the other, which could happen if we were still in our dream. Rather, it is to be done as partners, sharing information about our experience, without judgment or blame, in order to gain a better perspective of what occurred, and how we might handle a similar situation more effectively in the future.

In a practice of awakening, withdrawal is only used to support our intent to not participate in a reactive trance when one partner appears unable or unwilling to disengage. It is only a temporary action that allows us to disengage from an interaction we believe is destructive. It should never be presented as a withdrawal of love, or as a threat about the future. It is simply a last resort response to the needs of the present moment.

An Interactive Practice in Perspective

A shared practice of awakening is not a competition. It is about our mutual intent to cultivate our own capacity, and to assist one another in waking up. It is not about forcing or demanding that anyone wakes up. Therefore, we should only offer a wake-up nudge if we, ourselves, are clearly awake in that moment. If, at any point, we begin to feel reactive, such as feeling the impulse to defend or justify ourselves, or to criticize or attack our partner, we should not attempt to awaken them at that time. Our own trance will undoubtedly contaminate our interaction, and will no longer be motivated by simple, honest compassion. This would inevitably reinforce the intensity of the dream itself.

> A shared practice of awakening is not a competition. It is about our mutual intent to cultivate our own capacity, and to assist one another in waking up.

Instead, should we ever find ourselves troubled or disturbed by our partner's apparent lack of skill or commitment to our interactive practice, rather than trying to make that point to our partner, it is more appropriate to redirect our attention to ourselves and ask the central question, "Am I, in this moment, awake?" This is never intended to be a rhetorical question. It is a real question that calls for a genuine and careful response, a response that will lead us—sometimes gradually, sometimes immediately—back to a fully present and awake state of awareness. Only then will we have the clarity to offer a real gift of remembering who we both truly are to our beloved partner.

Key Points of Stage Two

Stage two is distinct in that it is the arena of everyday life where we are learning to apply and integrate steps one, two, and three from stage one of our interactive practice of awakening.

1. Seek to maintain a humble and fluid stance that is both active and receptive, with the genuine intent to:
   - offer a wake-up nudge (exactly as requested) only when we are awake
   - receive and acknowledge our partner's wake-up nudge when offered
2. Should our partner not be immediately receptive to our wake-up nudge, remember:
   - a wake-up nudge is only an offer, never a demand
   - it is our partner who is caught in their trance and suffering, not us
   - our only legitimate motive is compassion
3. If we find that we are attached to, or in need of, our partner waking up, remember:
   - this is our cue that we are in a trance
   - now is not the time to offer a wake-up nudge
4. Any time we become aware that we are slipping into our own reactive trance:
   - say so, openly and humbly
   - temporarily disengage from the interaction
   - voice our commitment to return to the conversation after re-connecting with our awake self
   - honor that commitment!
5. Always keep in mind:
   - our primary relationship is with the person that our partner truly is, not their trance identity
   - learning to stay awake when our beloved is not able to join us in that state is central to our practice

Conclusion

Ultimately, we will not have to go through the formality of following in a linear manner all the steps, levels, and stages of this practice. Once the levels and preparatory steps of stage one have been thoroughly integrated into our relationship, they will become the implicit background for stage two, where we will spend more of our time continuing to learn about waking up within and from our dream. In time, we will discover subtleties and nuances to our practice that will delight and nourish us along the way. We will find ourselves able to shift more quickly into an awake state of consciousness and to live more fully in the present moment. But prior to our mastering these practices, we may have some misgivings.

When I incorporate a practice of awakening in the course of therapy with couples, two concerns are commonly expressed. The first has to do with feeling overwhelmed or discouraged about one's own part in the practice. This occurs when a person has learned to recognize most of their trances and has had a certain degree of success in shifting their awareness. The difference in how they feel when they actually wake up is so remarkable that the pain of not waking up seems intensified. They might come into my office saying something to the effect of, "I thought I was learning how to wake up from my trances, but last week we had an argument and all my work went to hell! I feel like I've gone backwards in my growth. I am no better off now than I have ever been. This is either too hard, or I'm just too stupid to get it!"

In time, we will discover subtleties and nuances to our practice that will delight and nourish us along the way. We will find ourselves able to shift more quickly into an awake state of consciousness and to live more fully in the present moment.

At this point, I remind them that their perspective of their own growth (or lack thereof) is coming from the trance itself. A trance that, by definition, will always feel the same, *every single time they enter it.* It is not that they have gone backward in their growth. Rather, the journey of awakening has moments of lucidity and moments of entrancement. They have simply entered the trance again, and will certainly suffer as a result. But the instant—and I do mean the instant—we wake up, our suffering will end, and we will have the perspective to realize the significant progress we have made along the way.

The second concern has to do with one person feeling a sense of inequity, as though they carry most of the weight of the practice and are doing more than their fair share of the work. A typical question might be, "Why do I always have to be the one to keep initiating our practice?" or, "Why do I have to be the one who wakes up first?" Of course, this question is asked while one is identified with their trance and reflects issues that are part of its content, which could be anything from victimhood to martyrdom. They are confusing the act of waking up with the issues they are struggling with in their own waking dream.

The only real answer to the question, "Why do I have to be the one who wakes up first?" is, "You don't. Waking up is a choice, not an obligation." But once we understand that it is not the contents of the dream that cause the suffering, but the state of consciousness we are caught in, the question no longer makes sense. It would be the same as asking, "Why do I have to be the one to become free of my suffering first?" as if ending our own suffering is somehow unfair!

The instant—and I do mean the instant—we wake up, our suffering will end, and we will have the perspective to realize the significant progress we have made along the way.

The benefits of our growing capacity to wake up into the present moment are both immediate and far-reaching. Since our emotional suffering is for the most part due to our being trapped in a trance pattern of fear and resistance, by waking up from our trances as soon as they arise, we are learning to free ourselves from suffering. Having become identified with our individual and shared trances, our practice of awakening enables us to shed our trance identities and discover a far deeper and truer experience of who we are. Embracing this deeper, more essential Self allows us to access qualities of peace, joy, and love intrinsic to our soul, far beyond anything we could ever attain at a more superficial or reactive level.

It is from this place that we will be able to transform our relationship from the static patterns, needs, and limitations that have defined us into a fluid, elegant, mutually respectful, and profoundly intimate partnership of growth, healing, love, and freedom.

Bibliography

Beattie, Melody. *Co-Dependent No More*. New York: Hazelden, 1992.

Castaneda, Carlos. *The Art of Dreaming*. New York: HarperCollins, 1993.

Forward, Susan, and Donna Frazier. *Emotional Blackmail: When the People in Your Life Use Fear, Obligation, and Guilt to Manipulate You*. New York: HarperCollins, 1997.

Gangaji. *The Diamond in Your Pocket: Discovering Your True Radiance*. Boulder, CO: Sounds True, 2005.

Godwin, Malcolm. *The Lucid Dreamer: A Waking Guide for the Traveler Between Worlds*. UK: Labyrinth Publishing, 1994.

Kingma, Daphne Rose. *The Future of Love: The Power of the Soul In Intimate Relationships*. New York: Doubleday, 1998.

Krishnamurti, J. *The Only Revolution*. New York: Harper & Row, 1970.

——. *The Awakening of Intelligence*. New York: Harper & Row, 1973.

Levine, Stephen, and Ondrea Levine. *Embracing the Beloved: Relationship as a Path of Awakening*. New York: Doubleday, 1995.

Norwood, Robin. *Women Who Love Too Much: When You Keep Wishing and Hoping He'll Change, 2nd Edition*. Camarillo, CA: Devorss & Co., 2008.

Rossi, Ernest Lawrence. *The Psychobiology of Mind-Body Healing: New Concepts of Therapeutic Hypnosis*. New York: W.W. Norton and Company, 1986.

Ruiz, Don Miguel. *The Four Agreements: A Practical Guide to Personal Freedom, A Toltec Wisdom Book*. Carlsbad, CA: Hay House, 1997.

Suzuki, Shunryu Roshi. *Zen Mind, Beginner's Mind.* New York: Weatherhill Publishing, 1970.

Tolle, Eckhart. *A New Earth: Awakening to Your Life's Purpose.* New York: Plume, 2006.

——. *The Power of Now: A Guide to Spiritual Enlightenment.* Novato, CA: New World Library, 1999.

Welwood, John. *Journey of the Heart: The Path of Conscious Love.* New York: Harper Perennial, 1996.

——. *Love and Awakening: Discovering the Sacred Path of Intimate Relationship.* New York: Harper Paperbacks, 1997.

Wolinsky, Stephen, and Margaret Ryan. *Trances People Live: Healing Approaches in Quantum Psychology.* Las Vegas, NV: Bramble Books, 1991.

Wolinsly, Stephen Ph.D. *The Dark Side of the Inner Child: The Next Step.* Las Vegas, NV: Bramble Books,1993.

Suggested Reading List

(In addition to the bibiography):

Awakening Oriented or Expanded Perspectives on Relationships

Healing the War Between the Genders: The Power of the Soul-Centered Relationship. Linda Marks

The Bridge Across Forever: A True Love Story. Richard Bach

Meditative Consciousness, Mindfulness, Awake and Present Oriented Awareness/Perspective:

Virtually any of the nearly 50 publications by J. Krishnamurti including: *Commentaries on Living: Volumes I, II,* and *III*; *Think on These Things; Truth is a Pathless Land*

A Path with Heart: A Guide Through the Perils and Promises of Spiritual Life. Jack Kornfield

Wherever You Go, There You Are: Mindfulness Meditation in Everyday Life. Jon Kobat-Zinn

Hearts On Fire: The Tao of Meditation. Stephen H. Wolinsky, Ph.D.

Swallowing the Avocado of Enlightenment: A Spiritual Guide for the Rest of Us. Stephen Whiteman

Chodron, Pema. *Don't Bite the Hook: Finding Freedom from Anger, Resentment, and Other Destructive Emotions*. CD-ROM Series. Shambhala Audio Book: ISBN 978-1-59030-434-1. Distributed by Random House, Inc., 2007.

Glossary of Terms

Adapted/adaptive style of interaction: a particular way or style of interpersonal interaction that was originally a defensive adaptation to an emotionally threatening experience and has become incorporated into one's general repertoire of relating.

Age-regressed trance: a reactive trance formed at an earlier age that has remained frozen developmentally. When we enter such a trance, we are reactivating the qualities and felt sense of the original experience, almost as if we are reliving it. We feel, perceive, and interact through the lens of the earlier age. The wounded, or troubled, or powerless "inner child" exemplifies an age-regressed trance.

Awake state: a state of consciousness in which we are present and alert to our external environment and circumstance, as well as our internal experience, in contrast to a trance or dream state.

Awareness: the ever-present universal, irreducible, indivisible, non-specific underlying principle out of which specific and subjective consciousness emerges. Awareness is pre-conscious and pre-cognitive. While we can direct our attention and expand our consciousness to invite and allow greater awareness to be present to us, it can never be confined or bound to any particular state of consciousness. Awareness might well be the great frontier where science and spirituality, psychology, and mysticism ultimately find common ground.

Avoidant trance: a reactive trance (or defense mechanism) that functions to redirect our attention away from an emotionally painful or vulnerable experience. Often originated in, and associated with, painful experience in childhood.

Cellular memory: the kinesthetic or "felt sense" of a prior experience, often associated with a past traumatic experience. A reactivation of the physical and/or sensory aspect of a prior experience.

Consciousness: a specific and subjective form and structure of awareness. "Consciousness" is sometimes casually used synonymously with "awareness." While they are interrelated and sometimes overlapping, the distinction we make is that awareness is universal and non-specific, whereas consciousness is discrete, subjective, and specific. Consciousness is, therefore, always state bound, whereas awareness is ever-present but not bound to any particular state of consciousness. By way of analogy, if awareness represents "music," consciousness represents a particular "song"; if awareness is the totality of all water, consciousness is a particular bucket full, which limits, localizes, and provides a shape to a small portion of that water.

Complementary dysfunctional patterns: interactive trance patterns in which aspects of one person's trance complements those of the other person, generally manifesting as "paired bonds," such as teacher/student, emotional parent/emotional child, avoider/pursuer, abuser/victim, or alcoholic/enabler.

Consensus reality: a collectively agreed-upon composite of explicit and implicit beliefs, assumptions, and perceptions about reality. Consensus reality is a constructed and relative reality, informed by a multitude of elements, including scientific, religious, sociological, psychological, and neurological influences. Consensus reality may vary between cultures and periods of history. For instance, consensus reality once held that the world was flat.

Dreamed consciousness: the consciousness that is formed and maintained while dreaming.

Dysfunctional patterns of interaction: any psychological or behavorial dysfunction that is exhibited in an interpersonal interaction. (*See* psychological dysfunction)

Ego: a psychological mechanism whose primary function is to select, edit, interpret, and organize information and sensory data into a coherent experience of reality. The ego can be said to represent the form and structure of individual consciousness. It is rooted in our physical, cultural, and social existence. It operates by way of elaborate and multi-faceted interactions between the perceptions of the five physical senses, a full range of emotional responses, and a host of cognitive operations, such as association and memory, conditioning, and reasoning.

Ego consciousness: an aspect of consciousness exclusively derived from, defined by, and limited to, the parameters of the mechanisms and functions of the ego.

Ego control: refers to the strong tendency for us to think and act in such a way as to protect, justify, and reinforce our own image of ourselves.

Ego identity: our own image, belief, and sense of self formed by, and limited to, the mechanisms and functions of the ego.

Ego states: specific states of consciousness within the parameters of ego function.

Ego trances: All trances are sub-structures of the ego. The use of this term is for emphasis of that fact.

Ego defenses: any psychological mechanisms, such as denial, avoidance, intellectualization, distraction, rationalization, or reactive trances designed to protect, defend, or to justify, confirm, or validate our own personal reality as constructed by the ego.

Full present awareness: the experience of opening our mind to become deeply, acutely, and exquisitely aware of all that is within our external environment and internal experience in the present moment—without that awareness being filtered by the pre-conditioned perceptions, judgments, and beliefs of the ego.

Hypnotic trance: formal term for a specialized state of consciousness characterized by the withdrawal of our attention from full present awareness and a simultaneous redirection and fixation of attention to a narrower pattern of perception, feeling, and sensation, often but not always giving us the impression of "going deeply within" our own inner experience. Traditional Western psychology once limited the use of this term to refer to those states achieved by way of formal hypnotic inductions. However, contemporary thought has expanded the term to include spontaneous, "everyday" trances.

Lucid dream: a phenomenon that occurs when we are asleep and dreaming, and some aspect of our awareness becomes conscious of the fact that we are dreaming while still in the dream. This phenomenon exemplifies the natural capacity to access two different states of consciousness simultaneously. Because of this, we are able to incorporate this same capacity in our practice of "waking up" in relation to our trances.

Perceptual innocence: direct, unfiltered, immediate perception free of any kind of social, cultural, psychological, philosophical, or intellectual bias.

Present moment: the immediate moment in time—in contrast to "past" or "future"; the temporal state referred to as "now," or "this instant," or "this moment."

Present-oriented: any experience or state of consciousness which is oriented to the present moment.

Post-traumatic stress: a form of psychological distress related to a prior traumatic experience or event. Extreme cases of post traumatic stress can crystallize into a dysfunctional trance pattern commonly referred to as Post-Traumatic Stress Disorder, which manifests in a variety of psychological and behavioral symptoms and can trigger the internal experience of "re-living" the original trauma.

Psychological dysfunction: any psychological or behavioral pattern that is comprised of: 1. a false premise about the present moment (though it may have had historical validity); 2. personal awareness that is significantly limited or distorted; and 3. feelings, perceptions, and reactions that occur automatically according to a pre-established pattern.

Psychological entrancement: the process or condition of being drawn into a trance.

Reactive trance: a hypnotic trance (usually fearful or painful and self-protective) automatically triggered by an event or circumstance, an interpersonal encounter, or an image, memory, or sensory experience that is negatively emotionally charged.

Shared waking dream: can be used synonymously with "interactive trance," but usually implies a longer sustained interactive trance or composite of such trances.

Soul: the spiritual essence and quality of a person. Transpersonal, spiritual, or true Self in contrast to our ego identity. An individualized expression of Spirit or Universal Being (much like a wave of an ocean).

Spiritual awakening: the direct experiential realization of our sacred, transcendent, and essential Self or Being. Implied in this is the recognition that all relative or subjective experience of self and the world (physical, psychological, social, and cultural) is transient and relative, and does not represent absolute truth.

Spiritual bypass: term used in transpersonal psychology to describe the denial, avoidance, minimizing, or by-passing of unhealed or unresolved psychological or interpersonal issues while seeking or trying to maintain a more advanced, elevated, or transcendent spiritual experience.

State of consciousness: the experiential quality, dimension, and pattern of energy, sensation, and perception that shapes, limits, contains, and expresses consciousness in a given moment.

State-bound learning and memory: a term referring to the association of knowledge, skills, and kinesthetic learning to a specific state of consciousness, so that our ability to easily access and accurately remember what we once learned is greatly enhanced by, if not dependent upon, re-entering the specific state of consciousness in which the learning originally took place.

Trance: a specialized state of consciousness characterized by the withdrawal of our attention from full present awareness and a simultaneous redirection and fixation of attention to a narrower pattern of perception, feeling, and sensation, often but not always giving us the impression of "going deeply within" our own inner experience.

Trance consciousness: the full range of our subjective experience of reality (i.e., thoughts, feelings, perceptions) within a trance.

Trance identity: the specialized experience of self—specific to, and confined within, a particular trance.

Trance pattern: the repetitive and automatic configuration of thoughts, feelings, assumptions, perceptions, reactions, and behaviors specific to a particular trance.

Trance reaction: an automatic emotional or behavioral reaction precipitated by, or occurring within, a trance.

Trance state: a specialized state of consciousness characterized by the withdrawal of our attention from full present awareness and a simultaneous redirection and fixation of attention to a narrower pattern of perception, feeling, and sensation, often but not always giving the impression of "going deeply within" our own inner experience. Synonymous with "Trance."

Trigger: any precipitating event, circumstance, sensory experience, memory, or interaction that activates a trance.

Unconditioned awake presence: the experience of opening our mind to become deeply, acutely, and exquisitely aware of all that is within our external environment and internal experience in the present moment—without that awareness being filtered by the pre-conditioned perceptions, judgments, and beliefs of the ego. Can be used synonymously with "full present awareness" but with the emphasis on its unconditioned aspect.

Unconscious: a noun in psychodynamic theory that refers to an inner region of the psyche where repressed or otherwise unavailable memories, urges, etc., reside, as in "the unconscious." It can also be used as an adjective to simply mean something we are not consciously aware of, such as "an unconscious anger."

Unhealed emotional wounds: any of a wide range of emotional hurts, assaults, betrayals, or traumas of the past that have not healed or been resolved and therefore continue to impact us. Unhealed emotional wounds are often the source of reactive trances.

Waking dream: can be used synonymously with " trance," but usually implies a longer sustained trance or composite of such trances.

Zen-like: Zen is a sect of Buddhism that emphasizes direct perception of reality without any intermediary thoughts, pre-conceptions, assumptions, expectations, or conditioning. Therefore, a true experience of Zen always will be profoundly original. The Zen teacher Shunryu Suzuki Roshi addressed this in his book *Zen Mind, Beginner's Mind.* An inherent aspect of Zen consciousness is perceptual innocence.

Waking Up Tools at a Glance

Six Characteristics of Trance States 120

Key Points of an Individual Practice 122

Key Points of a Parallel Practice 123

Three Steps of an Interactive Practice of Awakening
Stage One: Preparation 124

An Interactive Practice, Stage Two: Application 126

Six Characteristics of Trance States

1. A trance state generally manifests as a specific and discrete pattern of consciousness that acts as a temporary filter or lens of perception. Thoughts, feelings, events and sensory data are all selected, edited, interpreted, and categorized in order to be congruent with the particular lens through which we are perceiving our environment. Because of this, trance realities tend to be self-confirming, even when full present awareness would likely elicit a markedly different perception.
2. While fully immersed in a trance state, we only have access to the resources—knowledge, skills, choices, perceptions, emotional repertoire—that are part of the trance state itself.
3. Once a trance is engaged, it tends to remain intact until it runs its full course or is interrupted.
4. A trance that holds emotional significance for an individual, and recurs many times, will develop its own familiar content, rhythm, texture and feeling tone, all of which is reactivated every time the trance is engaged. The subjective experience that is created and uniquely attuned to a particular state tends to solidify, through time and repetition, into a specialized experience of self generally referred to as a trance identity. Entering a trance becomes synonymous with taking on, or fusing with, that identity.
5. Once a trance pattern has been established, it may temporarily recede from our conscious awareness into a relatively dormant or inactive state. A trance pattern is comprised of a variety of intricately associated elements of an experience. These elements could include the situation or event, any thoughts, emotions, or interactions that accompanied the experience, and any related physical movements, sensations, sights, sounds, or smells that may have been part of the total experience. Any single element or combination of elements experienced at another time could activate or trigger—by association—the re-emergence of the entire trance experience.

6. Because a trance state is a contraction of consciousness away from full present awareness, we no longer have full present awareness as an immediate basis for contrast and perspective. Therefore, while we are in a hypnotic trance, we generally will not realize it. In retrospect, we may well recognize the trance we were in. But while in the trance, it was the only reality we were aware of.

Key Points of an Individual Practice

1. **Recognition:**
   a. Initially, keep a journal or notebook to identify as many trances as possible within a given period of time (a day, a weekend, a week).
   b. Look for and note:
      - the entrance (or triggering event)
      - the primary emotion or feeling tone and theme
      - the exit (or circumstance that facilitated a return to full present awareness)

2. **Observation:**
   a. Bring our attention to the witness aspect of our awareness.
      - The witness is non-judging, non-attached, and has no need to change or resist our experience within the trance.
   b. From the witness state, carefully observe the trance as it unfolds, just as if lucid dreaming.
      - Watch the patterns of thought, feelings, assumptions, judgments, and reactions of the trance state identity.

3. **Shifting:**
      - Shifting is a natural occurrence that begins when we are aware of both our trance and the witness simultaneously.
   a. Do not try to resist, overcome, or get rid of the trance (this would only further imbed us in it, like struggling in quicksand).
   b. Remember that a trance functions as a distorted lens of perception that selects, edits, interprets, and categorizes all information and sensory data according to its own patterns. Therefore, do not give the trance experience credibility for accurately representing an *objective* reality.
   c. Bring more and more attention to the activity of observing, gradually shifting the "weight" of personal identification from the trance identity to the observing Self.
   d. Offer loving forgiveness to the trapped aspect of ourselves as long as it continues to be ensnared in its trances, or waking dreams.

Key Points of a Parallel Practice

The purpose of a parallel practice is to create a safe space (and process) where you and your partner are able to be vulnerable and transparent with each other with no need to defend or justify yourselves.

1. Establish a mutually agreed upon frequency, time, and place for the exclusive purpose of engaging in a parallel practice.
   - Once or twice a week seems best suited for most couples initially
   - A set amount of time, 45 min. to 1 hour for each meeting, is helpful
   - A time when neither are depleted or distracted
   - A place where both feel safe and secure
2. Take turns sharing with each other the successes, challenges, and surprises of your ongoing individual practices.
   - Use this sharing to help fine-tune your skills of recognizing, observing, and shifting in relation to your own trances.
3. Listen to your partner's experience without critiquing, "helping," or teaching.
   - Questions for clarification and empathetic or congratulatory responses only!
4. Initially, talk only about those trances that do not directly involve your relationship.

Three Steps of an Interactive Practice of Awakening Stage One: Preparation

Step One

1. Bring your attention fully to the present moment.
2. Acknowledge your intent to know and to be known by your partner at the level of your souls.
3. Take time together to sift through trance identifications, and the historical circumstances and issues of your personal stories, to discern and behold your deeper, truer selves in the present moment.
4. Acknowledge your own responsibility and personal commitment to continuing your individual practice of awakening, incorporating the skills of recognition, observation, and shifting.
5. Declare your mutual intent to offer and receive support and assistance in waking up together in a spirit of love, humility, and non-competition.

Step Two

1. Together, identify, name, and list all ongoing or repeated shared trances.
2. Earmark the more emotionally charged or challenging trances, and start mapping the parameters of the less "risky" trances first in order to build more skill and confidence before progressing to the more challenging trances.
3. Map out the parameters of each trance, including:
   a. the triggering event or circumstance
   b. the sequence and style of our interaction
   c. each partner's role in the trance
   d. the primary emotional qualities and reactions of each role

Step Three

1. Each partner chooses a comment, phrase, or question to serve as a personalized wake-up cue.
2. Each shares the exact words, tone of voice, and gestures (if relevant) that would most likely and readily be received as a friendly, non-challenging, wake-up nudge.
3. Each repeats back exact words, tone of voice, and gestures (if any) and tweak as necessary until it feels just right to our partner.
4. Each partner writes down exact comment (for safe-keeping and later reference) and agrees not to change or improvise when using.
5. Both promise to offer a wake-up nudge only in a spirit of compassion, humility, and non-attachment to our partner's response (i.e., never while we are in a trance state).
6. Both promise that when our partner offers us our wake-up nudge, we will do our very best to honor our agreement to receive it in the spirit in which it is being offered.

An Interactive Practice
Stage Two: Application

Step four is distinct in that it is the arena of everyday life where we are learning to apply and integrate steps one, two, and three from stage one of our interactive practice of awakening.

1. Seek to maintain a humble and fluid stance that is both active and receptive, with the genuine intent to:
   - offer a wake-up nudge (exactly as requested) only when we are awake
   - receive and acknowledge our partner's wake-up nudge when offered
2. Should our partner not be immediately receptive to our wake-up nudge, remember:
   - a wake-up nudge is only an offer, never a demand
   - it is our partner who is caught in their trance and suffering, not us
   - our only legitimate motive is compassion
3. If we find that we are attached to, or in need of, our partner waking up, remember:
   - this is our cue that we are in a trance
   - now is not the time to offer a wake-up nudge
4. Any time we become aware that we are slipping into our own reactive trance:
   - say so, openly and humbly
   - temporarily disengage from the interaction
   - voice our commitment to return to the conversation after re-connecting with our awake self
   - honor that commitment!
5. Always keep in mind:
   - our primary relationship is with the person that our partner truly is, not their trance identity
   - learning to stay awake when our beloved is not able to join us in that state is central to our practice

About the Author

Leland "Chip" Baggett, M.A., LPC, received a Master's degree in Humanistic Psychology from the University of West Georgia in 1977. He is past president of the North Carolina Mental Health Counselors Association (1982–1983), past president of the Association For Humanistic Psychology (2001–2002), and co-president of the Association For Humanistic Psychology (2009–2010). In addition to maintaining a private psychotherapy practice for nearly three decades, Chip has served as a consultant, national speaker, and workshop presenter on topics that integrate psychological, interpersonal, and spiritual dimensions of being. His areas of expertise and experience range from, "Parenting as a Spiritual Practice," "Radical Intimacy," and "Spiritual Emergencies," to a variety of professional trainings in humanistic, existential, and transpersonal approaches to counseling and psychotherapy.

In 1988 Chip wrote a book of poetry, *So Where's The Dawn,* which depicts the journey of emotional healing after the loss of a relationship. He currently resides in Asheville, North Carolina, where he continues to work with individuals, couples, and groups. Using the material contained in this book, Chip also offers a series of experiential workshops for couples.

For more information, visit wakinguptogether.net, or contact the author at: leland@wakinguptogether.net.

The following page contains perforated quick-reference guides for you and your partner. You can use the top two to carry with you, and the bottom one to post on your fridge, mirror, or anywhere you will see frequently throughout the day. You may find these handy portable references very helpful as you incorporate this new practice.